The Buddhist Teaching on Physical Phenomena

Nina van Gorkom

2008

First edition published in 2008 by
Zolag
32 Woodnook Road
Streatham
London
SW16 6TZ
www.zolag.co.uk

ISBN 978-1-897633-25-0
Copyright Nina van Gorkom
All rights reserved
British Library Cataloguing in Publication Data
A CIP record for this book is available from the British Library
Printed in the UK and USA by Lightningsource.

Contents

Preface		iii
Introduction		ix
1	The Four Great Elements	1
2	The Eight Inseparables	13
3	The Sense-Organs	21
4	Sense Objects	31
5	Subtle Rūpas and Kamma	39
6	Intimation	47
7	Rūpas from different Factors	55
8	Characteristics of all Rūpas	61
9	Groups of Rūpas	71
10	Conclusion	77
Glossary		81

Preface

> That which is made of iron, wood or hemp is not a strong bond, say the wise; (but) that longing for jewels, ornaments, children and wives is far greater an attachment.
>
> Dhammapada (vs. 345).

Attachment to people and possessions is strong, almost irresistible. We are infatuated by what we see, hear, smell, taste, experience through the bodysense and through the mind. However, all the different things we experience do not last. We lose people who are dear to us and we lose our possessions. We can find out that attachment leads to sorrow, but at the moments of attachment we do not want to accept the truth of the impermanence of all things. We want pleasant objects for ourselves, and we consider the "self" the most important thing in the world.

Through the Buddhist teachings we learn that what we take for "self", for "our mind" and for "our body", consists of changing phenomena. That part of the Buddhist teachings which is the "Abhidhamma" enumerates and classifies all phenomena of our life: mental phenomena or nāma and physical phenomena or rūpa. Seeing is nāma, it experiences visible object through the eye-door. Visible object or colour is rūpa, it does not experience anything. The eyesense, that functions as the eye-door through which visible object is experienced, is also rūpa. The rūpas that are sense objects, namely, visible object, sound, smell, flavour and tangible object, and also the rūpas that are the sense organs of eyes, ears, nose, tongue and bodysense, are conditions for the nāmas to experience objects. Nāma and rūpa are interrelated.

Nāma and rūpa are ultimate realities. We should know the difference between ultimate truth and conventional truth. Conventional truth is the world of concepts such as person, tree or animal. Before we learnt about Buddhism, conventional truth, the world of concepts, was the only truth we knew. It is useful to examine the meaning of concept, in Pāli: paññatti. The word concept can stand for the name or term that conveys an idea and it can also stand for the idea itself conveyed by a term. Thus, the name "tree" is a concept, and also the idea we form up of "tree" is a concept. When we touch what we call a tree, hardness, which is a kind of rūpa can be experienced. Through the eyes only the rūpa that is visible object or colour can be experienced. Visible object and hardness are ultimate realities, paramattha dhammas, each with their own characteristic. These characteristics do not change, they can be experienced without having to name them. Colour is always colour, hardness is always hardness, even when we give them another name.

The whole day we touch things such as a fork, a plate or a chair. We believe that we know instantaneously what different things are, but after the sense-impressions such as seeing or the experiencing of tactile object through the bodysense, there are complicated processes of remembrance of former experiences and of classification, and these moments succeed one another very rapidly. Concepts are conceived through remembrance. We remember the form and shape of things, we know what different things are and what they are used for. We could not lead our daily life without conventional truth; we do not have to avoid the world of conventional truth. However, in between the moments of thinking of concepts, understanding of ultimate realities, of nāma and rūpa, can be developed. The development of understanding does not prevent us from doing all the chores of daily life, from talking to other people, from helping them or from being generous to them. We could not perform deeds of generosity if we would not think of conventional truth, such as the things we are giving or the person to whom we give. But through the development of understanding we shall learn to distinguish between absolute truth and conventional truth.

The "Abhidhammattha Sangaha", a compendium of the Abhidhamma composed in India at a later time[1], states that concepts are only shadows of realities. When we watch T.V., we see projected images of people and we know that through the eyesense only visible object is seen, no people. Also when we look at the persons we meet, only colour is experienced through the eyesense. In the ultimate sense there are no people. Although they seem very real, they are only shadows of what is really there. The truth is different from what we always assumed. What we take for a person are only nāmas and rūpas that arise and fall away. So long as we have not realized the arising and falling away of nāma and rūpa we continue to believe in a lasting self.

Ultimate realities are impermanent, they arise and fall away. Concepts are objects of thinking, they are not real in the ultimate sense. Nāma and rūpa, not concepts, are the objects of understanding. The purpose of the development of the eightfold Path is seeing ultimate realities as impermanent, suffering and non-self. If the difference between concepts and ultimate realities is not known, the eightfold Path cannot be developed. Right understanding, the leading factor of the eightfold Path, is developed through direct awareness of nāma and rūpa. However, this is difficult and it can only be learnt very gradually. When direct awareness arises of one object at a time as it appears through one of the senses or through the mind-door, we do not think of a concept of a "whole", of a person or thing, at that moment. The study of rūpas can help us to have more understanding of the sense objects and of the doorways of the senses through which these objects are experienced. If we do not have a foundation knowledge of objects and doorways we cannot know how to be

---

[1] This work has been ascribed to Anuruddha. It has been translated and published into English by the P.T.S. under the title of "Compendium of Philosophy", and by Ven. Nārada, Colombo, under the title of "A Manual of the Abhidhamma". It has also been translated by the Venerable Bikkhu Bodhi as "A Comprehensive Manual of Abhidhamma". Moreover, it has been translated together with its commentary as "Summary of the Topics of Abhidhamma" and "Exposition of the Topics of Abhidhamma", by R.P. Wijeratne and Rupert Gethin.

aware of one reality at a time as it appears at the present moment. The study of nāma and rūpa can be a condition for the arising of direct awareness later on.

The study of rūpas is not the study of physics or medical science. The aim of the understanding of nāma and rūpa is the eradication of the wrong view of self and freedom from enslavement to defilements. So long as one clings to an idea of self who owns things, it can give rise to avarice and jealousy which may even motivate bad deeds such as stealing or killing. Defilements cannot be eradicated immediately, but when we begin to understand that our life is only one moment of experiencing an object through one of the six doorways, the clinging to the idea of an abiding ego, of a person or self will decrease.

All three parts of the Buddha's teachings, namely the Vinaya (Book of Discipline for the monks), the Suttanta (Discourses) and the Abhidhamma point to the same goal: the eradication of defilements. From my quotations of sutta texts the reader can see that there is also Abhidhamma in the suttas, thus, that the teachings are one, the teaching of the Buddha. I have added questions at the end of each chapter in order to encourage the reader to check his understanding. I have used Pāli terms next to the English equivalents in order to help the reader to know the precise meaning of the realities explained in the Abhidhamma. The English terms have a specific meaning in the context of conventional use and they do not render the precise meaning of the reality represented by the Pāli term. The texts from which I have quoted, including the scriptures and the commentaries, have been translated into English by the Pāli Text Society.

The first of the seven books of the Abhidhamma, the "Dhammasangaṇi", translated as "Buddhist Psychological Ethics"[2], is a compilation of all nāma and rūpa, of all that is real. The source for my book on physical phenomena is that part of the "Dhammasangaṇi" which deals with this subject, as well as the commentary to this book, the "Atthasālinī", translated as "Expositor"[3], written by the

---
[2] Pali Text Society, reprint 1993.
[3] Pali Text Society, 1976.

venerable Buddhaghosa. I also used the "Visuddhimagga", translated as "The Path of Purification", an encyclopedia by the venerable Buddhaghosa[4].

I wish to express my deepest gratefulness to Ms Sujin Boriharnwanaket who always inspired me to verify the teachings in daily life. She reminded me never to forget the goal of the teachings: the development of understanding of all that appears through the sense-doors and the mind-door so that clinging to an idea of self and all defilements can be eradicated.

May this book on rūpas help the reader to develop right understanding of nāma and rūpa!

---

[4] I used the translation of Ven. Nyāṇamoli, 1964, Colombo, Sri Lanka. There is another translation by Pe Maung Tin under the title of "The Path of Purity", P.T.S.

Introduction

The Abhidhamma teaches us that in the ultimate sense our life is nāma and rūpa that arise because of their appropriate conditions and then fall away. What we take for person or self is citta[5] or consciousness, cetasika[6] or mental factors arising with the citta, and rūpa or physical phenomena. Citta and cetasika are nāma, they experience objects, whereas rūpa does not know anything. Citta experiences sense objects through the five senses. The sense objects as well as the sense organs are rūpas. The five senses by means of which cittas experience an object are called doors. When we think of something we saw or heard, citta does not experience an object through a sense-door but through another door: the mind-door. Thus there are six doorways. Through the mind-door citta can experience ultimate realities, nāma and rūpa, as well as concepts.

Citta experiences only one object and then it falls away to be succeeded by the next citta. We may have thought that there is one consciousness that lasts, that can see, hear and think, but this is not so. Only one citta arises at a time: at one moment a citta that sees arises, at another moment a citta that hears and at another moment again a citta that thinks. In our life an unbroken series of cittas arise in succession.

Cittas can be good or wholesome, kusala cittas, they can be unwholesome, akusala cittas, or they can be neither kusala nor akusala. Seeing, for example, is neither kusala nor akusala, it only experiences

---
[5]Pronounced as chitta.
[6]Pronounced as chetasika.

visible object through the eye-door. After seeing has fallen away, visible object is experienced by kusala cittas or by akusala cittas. Thus, when an object impinges on one of the six doors different types of cittas arise in a series or process and all of them experience that object. They arise in a specific order within the process and there is no self who can prevent their arising. The cittas that arise in a process experience an object through one of the five sense-doors and through the mind-door.

Only one citta arises at a time, but each citta is accompanied by several cetasikas or mental factors that share the same object with the citta but perform each their own function. Some cetasikas such as feeling and remembrance or "perception" (saññā) accompany each citta, others do not. Unwholesome mental factors, akusala cetasikas, only accompany akusala cittas, whereas "beautiful" mental factors, sobhana cetasikas, accompany kusala cittas.

As regards physical phenomena or rūpa, there are twentyeight kinds of rūpa in all. Rūpas are not merely textbook terms, they are realities that can be directly experienced. Rūpas do not know or experience anything; they can be known by nāma. Rūpa arises and falls away, but it does not fall away as quickly as nāma. When a characteristic of rūpa such as hardness impinges on the bodysense it can be experienced through the bodysense by several cittas arising in succession within a process. But even though rūpa lasts longer than citta, it falls away again, it is impermanent.

Rūpas do not arise singly, they arise in units or groups. What we take for our body is composed of many groups or units, consisting each of different kinds of rūpa, and the rūpas in such a group arise together and fall away together. The reader will come across four conditioning factors that produce rūpas of the body: kamma, citta, temperature and food. The last three factors are easier to understand, but the first factor, kamma, is harder to understand since kamma is a factor of the past. We can perform good and bad deeds through body, speech and mind and these can produce their appropriate results later on. Such deeds are called kamma, but when we are more precise kamma is actually the cetasika volition or intention (cetanā) that motivates the deed. Kamma is a mental activity which can be accumulated. Since cittas that arise and fall away succeed one another in an unbroken series, the force of kamma is carried on from one moment of citta to the next moment of citta, from one life to the next life. In this way kamma is capable to produce its result later on. A good deed, kusala kamma, can produce a pleasant result, and an evil deed can produce an unpleasant result. Kamma produces result at the first moment of life: it produces rebirth-consciousness in a happy plane of existence such as the human plane or a heavenly plane, or in an unhappy plane of existence such as a hell plane or the animal world. Throughout our life kamma produces seeing, hearing and the other sense-impressions that are vipākacittas, cittas that are results. Vipākacittas are neither kusala cittas nor akusala cittas. Seeing a pleasant object is the result of kusala kamma and seeing an unpleasant object is the result of akusala kamma. Due to kamma gain and loss, praise and blame alternate in our life.

Rebirth-consciousness is the mental result of kamma, vipākacitta, but at that moment kamma also produces rūpas and kamma keeps on producing rūpas throughout life; when it stops producing rūpas our life-span has to end. Kamma produces particular kinds of rūpas such as the senses, as we shall see. Citta also produces rūpas. Our different moods become evident by our facial expressions and then it is clear that citta produces rūpas. Temperature, which is actually the element of heat, also produces rūpas. Throughout life the element of heat produces rūpas. Nutrition is another factor that produces rūpas. When food has been taken by a living being it is assimilated into the body and then nutrition can produce rūpas. Some of the groups of rūpas of our body are produced by kamma, some by citta, some by temperature and some by nutrition. The four factors which produce the rūpas of our body support and consolidate each other and keep this shortlived body going. If we see the intricate way in which different factors condition the rūpas of our body we shall be less inclined to think that the body belongs to a self.

There are not only rūpas of the body, there are also rūpas which are the material phenomena outside the body. What we take for rocks, plants or houses are rūpas and these originate from temperature. We may wonder whether there are no other factors apart from the element of heat that contribute to the growth of plants, such as soil, light and moisture. It is true that these factors are the right conditions that have to be present so that a plant can grow. But what we call soil, light and moisture are, when we are more precise, different combinations of rūpas, none of which can arise without the element of heat or temperature that produces them. Rūpas outside the body are only produced by temperature, not by kamma, citta or nutrition.

Rūpas perform their functions, no matter one dresses oneself, eats, digests one's food, moves about, gesiticulates, talks to others, in short, during all one's activities. If we do not study rūpas we may not notice their characteristics that appear all the time in daily life. We shall continue to be deluded by the outward appearance of things instead of knowing realities as they are. We should remember that the rūpa which is the "earth- element" or solidity can appear as hardness or softness. Hardness impinges time and again on the bodysense, no matter what we are doing. When hardness appears it can be known as only a kind of rūpa, be it hardness of the body or hardness of an external object. In the ultimate sense it is only a kind of rūpa. The detailed study of nāma and rūpa will help us to see that there isn't anything that is "mine" or self. The goal of the study of the Abhidhamma is the development of wisdom leading to the eradication of all defilements.

Chapter 1

The Four Great Elements

Rūpas do not arise singly, they arise in units or groups. Each of these groups is composed of different kinds of rūpa. There are four kinds of rūpa, the four "Great Elements" (Mahā-bhūta rūpas), which have to arise together with each and every group of rūpas, no matter whether these are rūpas of the body or rūpas outside the body. The types of rūpa other than the four Great Elements depend on these four rūpas and cannot arise without them. They are the following rūpas:

the Element of Earth or solidity

the Element of Water or cohesion

the Element of Fire or heat

the Element of Wind (air) or motion

Earth, Water, Fire and Wind do not in this context have the same meaning as in conventional language, neither do they represent conceptual ideas as we find them in different philosophical systems. In the Abhidhamma they represent ultimate realities, specific rūpas each with their own characteristic. The element of earth, in Pāli: paṭhavī dhātu, translated into English as "solidity" or "extension", has the characteristic of hardness or softness. It can be directly experienced when we touch something hard or soft. We do not have to name the rūpa denoted by "element of earth" in order to experience it. It is an element that arises and falls away; it has no abiding substance, it is devoid of a "self". It may seem that hardness can last for some time, but in reality it falls away immediately. Rūpas are replaced so long as there are conditions for them to be produced by one of the four factors of kamma, citta, temperature or nutrition[1]. The hardness that is experienced now is already different from the hardness that arose a moment ago.

We used to think that a cushion or a chair could be experienced through touch. When we are more precise, it is hardness or softness that can be experienced through touch. Because of remembrance of former experiences we can think of a cushion or chair and we know that they are named "cushion" or "chair". This example can remind us that there is a difference between ultimate realities and concepts we can think of but which are not real in the ultimate sense.

Viewing the body and the things around us as different combinations of rūpas may be new to us. Gradually we shall realize that rūpas are not abstract categories, but that they are realities appearing in daily life. I shall quote the definitions of the different rūpas given by the "Visuddhimagga" and the "Atthasālinī". These definitions mention the characteristic, function, manifestation and proximate cause or immediate occasion[2] of the rūpas that are explained. The "Visuddhimagga" (XI,93)[3] gives, for example, the following definition of the rūpa that is the earth element or solidity:

> "... The earth element has the characteristic of hardness. Its function is to act as a foundation. It is manifested as receiving...."

Each reality has its own individual characteristic by which it can be distinguished from other realities. The earth element or solidity has hardness (or softness) as characteristic, the fire element has

---
[1] See Introduction. This will be explained further on.
[2] The Atthasālinī explains these terms in Book I, Part II, Analysis of Terms, 63.
[3] See also Dhammasangaṇi §648, and Atthasālinī II, Book II, Part I, Ch III, 332.

heat as characteristic. Such characteristics can be experienced when they appear. As to function, rūpas have functions in relation to other rūpas or in relation to nāma. Solidity acts as a foundation, namely for the other rūpas it arises together with in a group; that is its function. Smell, for example, could not arise alone, it needs solidity as foundation. It is the same with visible object or colour that can be experienced through the eyesense. Visible object or colour needs solidity as foundation or support, it could not arise alone. Solidity that arises together with visible object cannot be seen, only visible object can be seen. As regards manifestation, this is the way a reality habitually appears. Solidity is manifested as receiving, it receives the other rūpas it arises together with since it acts as their foundation. With regard to the proximate cause, according to the "Visuddhimagga" (XIV,35) each of the four Great Elements has the other three as its proximate cause. The four Great Elements arise together and condition one another.

At first the definitions of realities may seem complicated but when we have studied them, we shall see that they are helpful for the understanding of the different realities, and this includes understanding of the way they act on other realities and the way they manifest themselves. The study of realities is a foundation for the development of direct understanding, of seeing things as they really are.

In the "Greater Discourse on the Simile of the Elephant's Footprint" (Middle Length Sayings I, no. 28) we read that Sāriputta taught the monks about the four Great Elements. We read about the element of earth or solidity, which is translated here as "extension":

> " ... And what, your reverences, is the element of extension? The element of extension may be internal, it may be external. And what, your reverences, is the internal element of extension? Whatever is hard, solid, is internal, referable to an individual and derived therefrom, that is to say: the hair of the head, the hair of the body, nails, teeth, skin, flesh, sinews, bones, marrow of the bones, kidney, heart, liver, pleura, spleen, lungs,

intestines, mesentary, stomach, excrement, or whatever other thing is hard, solid, is internal..."

If the body can be seen as only elements, the wrong view of self can be eradicated. Solidity can be internal or external, outside the body. Solidity is also present in what we call a mountain or a rock, in all material phenomena. Sāriputta reminded the monks of the impermanence of the element of extension:

> "There comes a time, your reverences, when the element of extension that is external is agitated; at that time the external element of extension disappears. The impermanence of this ancient external element of extension can be shown, your reverences, its liability to destruction can be shown, its liability to decay can be shown, its liability to change can be shown. So what of this shortlived body derived from craving? There is not anything here for saying, 'I', or 'mine' or 'I am'..."

The impermanence of the element of solidity may manifest itself in such calamities of nature as an earthquake, but actually at each and every moment rūpas arise and then fall away, they do not last.

As regards the element of water (in Pāli: āpo dhātu) or cohesion, the "Visuddhimagga" (XI, 93) defines it as follows [4] :

> "... The water element has the characteristic of trickling. Its function is to intensify. It is manifested as holding together."

The element of water or cohesion cannot be experienced through the bodysense, only through the mind-door. When we touch what we call water, it is only solidity, temperature or motion which can be experienced through the bodysense, not cohesion. Cohesion has to arise together with whatever kind of materiality arises. It makes the other rūpas it accompanies cohere so that they do not become scattered. The "Atthasālinī" (II, Book II, Ch III, 335) explains:

---

[4]See also Dhammasangaṇi §652 and Atthasālinī II, Book II, Part I, Ch III, 332.

"... For the element of cohesion binds together iron, etc., in masses, makes them rigid. Because they are so bound, they are called rigid. Similarly in the case of stones, mountains, palm-seeds, elephant-tusks, ox-horns, etc. All such things the element of cohesion binds, and makes rigid; they are rigid because of its binding."

We read in the above quoted sutta that Sāriputta explained to the monks about the internal liquid element (element of water):

"... Whatever is liquid, fluid, is internal, referable to an individual or derived therefrom, that is to say: bile, phlegm, pus, blood, sweat, fat, tears, serum, saliva, mucus, synovial fluid, urine or whatever other thing is liquid, fluid, is internal ... "

When we shed tears or swallow saliva we can be reminded that what we take for the fluid of "my body" are only elements devoid of self. Sāriputta reminded the monks that the external liquid element can become agitated and can bring destruction to villages, towns, districts and regions, or that the water of the oceans may go down and disappear. It is liable to change and it is impermanent. Both the internal and the external liquid element are impermanent and not self.

As to the element of fire, heat or temperature (in Pāli: tejo dhātu), the "Visuddhimagga" (XI, 93) gives the following definition of it[5]:

"... The fire element has the characteristic of heat. Its function is to mature (maintain). It is manifested as a continued supply of softness[6]."

The element of heat or temperature can be experienced through the bodysense and it appears as heat or cold. Cold is a lesser degree

---

[5] See also Dhammasaṅgaṇi §648 and Atthasālinī II, Book II, Part I, Ch III, 332.
[6] The Atthasālinī (II, Book II, Part I, Ch III, 332) states that it has "the gift of softening (co-existent realities) as manifestation". It states: "When this body is accompanied by the life-controlling faculty, by the element of heat, by consciousness, then it becomes lighter, softer, more wieldy." In a corpse there is no body heat, it is stiff and not wieldy.

of heat. The element of heat accompanies all kinds of materiality that arises, rūpas of the body and materiality outside. It maintains or matures them. The element of heat is one of the four factors that produce rūpas of the body. At the first moment of life, kamma, a deed committed in the past, produces the rebirth-consciousness and also rūpa. After the rebirth-consciousness has arisen temperature also starts to produce rūpas of the body[7]. Rūpas which are materiality outside such as those of a plant or a rock are produced solely by temperature.

We read in the above quoted sutta that Sāriputta explained to the monks about the internal element of heat:

> "...Whatever is heat, warmth, is internal, referable to an individual and derived therefrom, such as by whatever one is vitalized, by whatever one is consumed, by whatever one is burnt up, and by whatever one has munched, drunk, eaten and tasted that is properly transmuted (in digestion), or whatever other thing is heat, warmth, is internal..."

The "Visuddhimagga" (XI, 36) which gives an explanation of the words of this sutta states that the element of heat plays its part in the process of ageing:

> "...whereby this body grows old, reaches the decline of the faculties, loss of strength, wrinkles, greyness, and so on."

As to the expression "burnt up", it explains that when one is excited the internal element of heat causes the body to burn. The element of heat also has a function in the digestion of food, it "cooks" what is eaten and drunk.

We may notice changes in body-temperature because of different conditions, for instance through the digestion of our food, or when we are excited, angry or afraid. So long as we are still alive the internal element of heat arises and falls away all the time. When heat

---

[7]This will be explained later on.

presents itself and when there is awareness of it it can be known as only a rūpa element, not "my body-heat". When we are absorbed in excitement, anger or fear we forget that there are in reality only different kinds of nāma and rūpa that arise and fall away.

The element of heat can be internal or external. Sāriputta explained that the liability to change of the external heat element and its impermanence can be seen when it becomes agitated and burns up villages, towns, districts and regions, and is then extinguished through lack of fuel. Both the internal and the external element of heat are impermanent and not self.

As to the element of wind (in Pāli: vāyo dhātu) or motion, the "Visuddhimagga" (XI, 93) defines it as follows[8] :

> "... The air element (wind) has the characteristic of distending. Its function is to cause motion. It is manifested as conveying[9]."

We may believe that we can see motion of objects but the rūpa which is motion cannot be seen. What we mean by motion as we express it in conventional language is not the same as the element of wind or motion. We notice that something has moved because of remembrance of different moments of seeing and thinking of what was perceived, but that is not the experience of the rūpa which is motion. This rūpa can be directly experienced through the bodysense. When we touch a body or an object with a certain resilience, the characteristic of motion or pressure may present itself. These are characteristics of the element of wind. It can also be described as vibration or oscillation. As we read in the definition, the function of the element of wind is to cause motion. It is, for example, a condition for the movement of the limbs of the body. However, we should not confuse pictorial ideas with the direct experience of this rūpa through the bodysense.

---

[8]See also Dhammasangaṇi §648 and Atthasālinī II, Book II, Part I, Ch III, 332.

[9]Taking from one point to another, Visuddhimagga XI, 93. The commentary explains: "Conveying is acting as cause for the successive arising at adjacent locations of the conglomeration of elements."

The element of wind or motion arises with all kinds of materiality, both of the body and outside the body. There is also motion with dead matter, such as a pot. It performs its function so that the pot holds its shape and does not collapse.

Sāriputta explained about the internal element of motion:

> "... And what, your reverences, is the internal element of motion? Whatever is motion, wind, is internal, referable to an individual and derived therefrom, such as winds going upwards, winds going downwards, winds in the abdomen, winds in the belly, winds that shoot across the several limbs, in-breathing, out-breathing, or whatever other thing is motion, wind, is internal..."

We may notice pressure inside the body. When its characteristic appears it can be known as only a rūpa that is conditioned. As to the words of the sutta, "winds that shoot across the several limbs", the "Visuddhimagga" (XI, 37) explains that these are: "winds (forces) that produce flexing, extending, etc., and are distributed over the limbs and the whole body by means of the network of veins (nerves)".

The element of wind plays its specific role in the strengthening of the body so that it does not collapse, and assumes different postures; it is a condition for the stretching and bending of the limbs. While we are bending or stretching our arms and legs the element of wind may appear as motion or pressure. We read in the "Visuddhimagga" (XI, 92):

> "The air element that courses through all the limbs and has the characteristic of moving and distending, being founded upon earth, held together by water, and maintained by fire, distends this body. And this body, being distended by the latter kind of air, does not collapse, but stands erect, and being propelled by the other (moving) air, it shows intimation, and it flexes and extends and it wriggles the hands and feet, doing so in the postures comprising walking, standing, sitting and

lying down. So this mechanism of elements carries on like a magic trick, deceiving foolish people with the male and female sex and so on."

We are deceived and infatuated by the outward appearance of a man or a woman and we forget that this body is a "mechanism of elements" and that it flexes and wriggles hands and feet, showing intimation by gestures or speech, because of conditions.

The above quoted sutta mentions, in connection with the element of wind, in-breathing and out-breathing. The "Visuddhimagga" (XI, 37) explains: "In-breath: wind in the nostrils entering in. Out-breath: wind in the nostrils issuing out." We are breathing throughout life, but most of the time we are forgetful of realities, we cling to an idea of "my breath". Breath is rūpa conditioned by citta and it presents itself where it touches the nosetip or upperlip. If there can be awareness of it, the characteristics of hardness, softness, heat or motion can be experienced one at a time. However, breath is very subtle and it is most difficult to be aware of its characteristic.

We read in the above quoted sutta that Sāriputta explained that the external element of motion can become agitated and carry away villages. Its liability to change and its impermanence can be seen. Both the external and the internal element of motion are impermanent.

As we have seen, the four great Elements always arise together, and each of them has the other three as its proximate cause. The "Visuddhimagga" (XI, 109) states that the four great Elements condition one another: the earth element acts as the foundation of the elements of water, fire and wind; the water element acts as cohesion for the other three Great Elements; the fire element maintains the other three Great Elements; the wind element acts as distension of the other three Great Elements.

We should remember that the element of water or cohesion cannot be experienced through the bodysense, only through the mind-door, and that the elements of earth, fire and wind can be directly experienced through the bodysense. The element of earth appears as hardness or softness, the element of fire as heat or cold and the element of wind as motion or pressure. Time and again rūpas such as hardness or heat impinge on the bodysense but we are forgetful of what things really are. We let ourselves be deceived by the outer appearance of things. The "Visuddhimagga" (XI, 100) states that the four Great Elements are "deceivers":

> "And just as the great creatures known as female spirits (yakkhinī) conceal their own fearfulness with a pleasing colour, shape and gesture to deceive beings, so too, these elements conceal each their own characteristics and function classed as hardness, etc., by means of a pleasing skin colour of women's and men's bodies, etc., and pleasing shapes of limbs and pleasing gestures of fingers, toes and eyebrows, and they deceive simple people by concealing their own functions and characteristics beginning with hardness and do not allow their individual essences to be seen. Thus they are great primaries (mahā-bhūta) in being equal to the great creatures (mahā-bhūta), the female spirits, since they are deceivers."

Realities are not what they appear to be. One may be infatuated by the beauty of men and women, but what one takes for a beautiful body are mere rūpa-elements.

The "Visuddhimagga" (XI, 98) states that the four Great Elements are like the great creatures of a magician who "turns water that is not crystal into crystal, and turns a clod that is not gold into gold..." We are attached to crystal and gold, we are deceived by the outward appearance of things. There is no crystal or gold in the ultimate sense, only rūpas which arise and then fall away.

We may be able to know the difference between the moments that we are absorbed in concepts and ideas and mindfulness of realities such as hardness or heat which appear one at a time. Mindfulness (sati) arises with kusala citta and it is mindful of one nāma or rūpa at a time. When we are, for example, stung by a mosquito, we may have aversion towards the pain and we may be forgetful of realities such as heat experienced at that moment through the bodysense. When there are conditions for kusala citta with mindfulness, whatever reality appears can be object of mindfulness. This is the way gradually to develop the understanding which knows nāma and rūpa as they are: only elements that are impermanent and devoid of self.

As we read in the "Greater Discourse of the Simile of the Elephant's Footprint", different "parts of the body", such as the hair of the head, the hair of the body, nails, teeth, skin, are mentioned where the characteristics of the four Great Elements are apparent. The aim is to see the body as it really is. When Sāriputta explained about the four Great Elements he repeated after each section:

> "... By means of perfect intuitive wisdom it should be seen of this as it really is, thus: This is not mine, this am I not, this is not myself..."

Questions

1. Can the element of water be experienced through touch?
2. Can the characteristic of motion be experienced through eyesense?
3. What is the proximate cause of each of the four Great Elements?

Chapter 2

The Eight Inseparable Rūpas

The four Great Elements of solidity, cohesion, temperature and motion are always present wherever there is materiality. Apart from these four elements there are other rūpas, namely twentyfour "derived rūpas" (in Pāli: upādā rūpas). The "Atthasālinī" (II, Book II, Ch III, 305) explains about them: "...grasping the great essentials (great elements), not letting go, such (derived rūpas) proceed in dependance upon them." Thus, the derived rūpas cannot arise without the four Great Elements.

Four among the derived rūpas always arise together with the four Great Elements in every group of rūpas and are thus present wherever materiality occurs, no matter whether rūpas of the body or materiality outside the body. These four rūpas are the following:

visible object (or colour)

odour

flavour

nutrition

The four Great elements and these four derived rūpas, which always arise together, are called the "inseparable rūpas" (in Pāli: avinibbhoga rūpas). Wherever solidity arises, there also have to be cohesion, temperature, motion, colour, odour, flavour and nutritive essence.

As regards visible object or colour, this is a rūpa that can be experienced through the eye-door. It is not a thing or a person. Visible object is the only rūpa that can be seen.

Colours are different because of different conditions[1] , but no matter what colour appears we should remember that what is experienced through the eye-door is the rūpa which is visible, visible object. The "Atthasālinī" (II, Book II, Ch III, 318) gives the following definition of visible object [2]:

> "... For all this matter has the characteristic of striking the eye, the function or property of being in relation of object to visual cognition, the manifestation of being the field of visual cognition, the proximate cause of the "four great essentials" (four Great Elements)."

Visible object has as its proximate cause the four Great Elements because it cannot arise without them. However, when a characteristic of one of these four Great Elements, such as hardness or heat, is experienced, the accompanying visible object cannot be experienced at the same time.

When there are conditions for seeing, visible object is experienced. When we close our eyes, there may be remembrance of the shape and form of a thing, but that is not the experience of visible object. The thinking of a "thing", no matter whether our eyes are closed or open, is different from the actual experience of what is visible.

We may find it difficult to know what visible object is, since we are usually absorbed in paying attention to the shape and form of things. When we perceive the shape and form of something, for example of a chair, we think of a concept. A chair cannot impinge on the eyesense. Seeing does not see a chair, it only sees what is visible. Seeing and thinking occur at different moments. We do

---

[1] See also Dhammasangaṇi §617.
[2] See also Visuddhimagga XIV, 54

not think all the time, also moments of just seeing arise, moments that we do not pay attention to shape and form. Only one citta at a time arises experiencing one object, but different experiences arise closely one after the other. When one cannot distinguish them yet from each other, one believes that they occur all at the same time. If we remember that visible object is the rūpa which can be experienced through the eyesense, right understanding of this reality can be developed.

As we have seen, odour is another rūpa among the eight inseparable rūpas. Wherever materiality occurs, no matter whether of the body or outside the body, there has to be odour. The "Dhammasangaṇi" (§ 625) mentions different odours, pleasant and unpleasant, but they all are just odour which can be experienced through the nose. The "Atthasālinī" (II, Book II, Ch III, 320) defines odour as follows[3] :

> "... all odours have the characteristic of striking the
> sense of smell, the property of being the object of
> olfactory cognition, the manifestation of being the field
> of the same..."

It has as proximate cause the four Great Elements. Odour cannot arise alone, it needs the four Great Elements which arise together with it and it is also accompanied by the other rūpas included in the eight inseparable rūpas. When odour appears we tend to be carried away by like or dislike. We are attached to fragrant odours and we loathe nasty smells. However, odour is only a reality which is experienced through the nose and it does not last. If one does not develop understanding of realities one will be enslaved by all objects experienced through the senses. On account of these objects akusala cittas tend to arise. If someone thinks that there is a self who can own what is seen, touched or smelt, he may be inclined to commit unwholesome deeds such as stealing. In reality all these objects are insignificant, they arise and then fall away immediately.

As regards flavour, the "Dhammasangaṇi" (§629) mentions different kinds of flavour, such as sour, sweet, bitter or pungent; they

---
[3]See also Visuddhimagga XIV, 56.

may be nice or nauseous, but they are all just flavour, experienced through the tongue. The "Atthasālinī" (II, Book II, Ch III, 320) defines flavour as follows[4] :

> "... all tastes have the characteristic of striking the tongue, the property of being the object of gustatory cognition, the manifestation of being the field of the same..."

Its proximate cause are the four Great Elements. Flavour does not arise alone, it needs the four Great Elements that arise together with it, and it is also accompanied by the other rūpas included in the eight inseparable rūpas. We are attached to food and we find its flavour very important. As soon as we have tasted delicious flavour, attachment tends to arise. We are forgetful of the reality of flavour which is only a kind of rūpa. When we recognize what kind of flavour we taste, we think about a concept, but this thinking is conditioned by the experience of flavour through the tongue.

Nutrition is another kind of rūpa which has to arise with every kind of materiality. It can be exerienced only through the mind-door. The "Dhammasangaṇi" (§646) mentions food such as boiled rice, sour gruel, flour, etc., which can be eaten and digested into the "juice" by which living beings are kept alive. The "Atthasālinī" (II, Book II, Ch III, 330) explains that there is foodstuff, the substance which is swallowed (kabaḷinkāro āhāro, literally, morsel-made food), and the "nutritive essence" (ojā). The foodstuff which is swallowed fills the stomach so that one does not grow hungry. The nutritive essence present in food preserves beings, keeps them alive. The nutritive essence in gross foodstuff is weak, and in subtle foodstuff it is strong. After eating coarse grain one becomes hungry after a brief interval. But when one has taken ghee (butter) one does not want to eat for a long time (Atthasālinī , 331).

The "Atthasālinī"(332) gives the following definition of nutriment[5] :

---
[4]See also Visuddhimagga XIV, 57
[5]See also Visuddhimagga XIV, 70

> "As to its characteristic, etc., solid food has the
> characteristic of nutritive essence, the function of
> fetching matter (to the eater), of sustaining matter as its
> manifestation, of substance to be swallowed as
> proximate cause."

Nutritive essence is not only present in rice and other foods, it is also present in what we call a rock or sand. It is present in any kind of materiality. Insects are able to digest what human beings cannot digest, such as, for example, wood.

Nutrition is one of the four factors which produce rūpas of the body. As we have seen, the other factors are kamma, citta and temperature [6]. In the unborn being in the mother's womb, groups of rūpa produced by nutrition arise as soon as the nutritive essence present in food taken by its mother pervades its body (Visuddhimagga XVII, 194). From then on nutrition keeps on producing rūpas and sustaining the rūpas of the body throughout life.

We can notice that nutrition produces rūpas when good or bad food affects the body in different ways. Bad food may cause the skin to be ugly, whereas the taking of vitamins for example may cause skin and hair to look healthy.

Because of attachment we tend to be immoderate as to food. We are not inclined to consider food as a medicine for our body. The Buddha exhorted the monks to eat just the quantity of food needed to sustain the body but not more and to reflect wisely when eating (Visuddhimagga I, 85). The monk should review with understanding the requisites he receives. We read in the "Visuddhimagga" (I, 124) about the right way of using the requisites (of robes, food, etc.):

> "... For use is blameless in one who at the time of
> receiving robes, etc., reviews them either as (mere)
> elements or as repulsive, and puts them aside for later
> use, and in one who reviews them thus at the time of
> using them."

---

[6]See Introduction.

The monk should review robes, and the other requisites of dwelling, food and medicines, as mere elements or as repulsive. If he considers food as repulsive it helps him not to indulge in it. Food consists merely of conditioned elements. This can be a useful reminder, also for laypeople, to be mindful when eating.

In the commentary to the "Satipaṭṭhāna Sutta"[7], in the section on Mindfulness of the Body, "Clear Comprehension in Partaking of Food and Drink", we read that, when one swallows food, there is no one who puts the food down into the stomach with a ladle or spoon, but there is the element of wind performing its function. We then read about digestion:

> "... There is no one who having put up an oven and lit a fire is cooking each lump standing there. By only the process of caloricity (heat) the lump of food matures. There is no one who expels each digested lump with a stick or pole. Just the process of oscillation (the element of wind or motion) expels the digested food."

There is no self who eats and drinks, there are only elements performing their functions.

Whatever kind of materiality arises, there have to be the four Great Elements and the four derived rūpas of visible object, odour, flavour and nutrition.

Because of ignorance we are attached to our possessions. We may understand that when life ends we cannot possess anything anymore. But even at this moment there is no "thing" we can possess, there are only different elements that do not stay. When we look at beautiful things such as gems we tend to cling to them. However, through the eyes only colour or visible object appears and through touch tangible object such as hardness appears. In the absolute sense it does not make any difference whether it is hardness of a gem or hardness of a pebble that is experienced through touch. We may not like to accept this truth since we find that gems and pebbles have

---

[7]The Papañcasūdanī. See "The Way of Mindfulness", a translation of the Satipaṭṭhāna Sutta, Middle Length Sayings I, 10, and its commentary, by Ven. Soma, B.P.S. Kandy.

different values. We have accumulated conditions to think about concepts and we neglect the development of understanding of realities; we tend to forget that what we call gems and also the cittas that enjoy them do not last, that they are gone immediately. Someone who leads the life of a layman enjoys his possessions, but he can also develop understanding of what things really are.

In the ultimate sense life exists only in one moment, the present moment. At the moment of seeing the world of visible object is experienced, at the moment of hearing the world of sound, and at the moment of touching the world of tangible object. Life is actually one moment of experiencing an object.

The "Book of Analysis"[8] (Part 3, Analysis of the Elements, §173) mentions precious stones together with pebbles and gravel in order to remind us of the truth. It explains about the internal element of extension (solidity) as being hair of the head, hair of the body and other "parts of the body". Then it explains about the external element of extension as follows:

> "Therein what is the external element of extension? That which is external, hard, harsh, hardness, being hard, external, not grasped. For example: iron, copper, tin, lead, silver, pearl, gem, cat's-eye, shell, stone, coral, silver coin, gold, ruby, variegated precious stone, grass, wood, gravel, potsherd, earth, rock, mountain; or whatever else there is..."

The elements give us pleasure or pain. When we do not realize them as they are, we are enslaved by them. We read in the "Kindred Sayings"(II, Nidāna-vagga, Ch XIV, Kindred Sayings on Elements, §34, Pain) that the Buddha said to the monks at Sāvatthī:

> "If this earth-element, monks, this water-element, this heat-element, this air-element were entirely painful, beset with pain, immersed in pain, not immersed in happiness, beings would not be lusting after them. But

---
[8]Vibhaṅga, Second Book of the Abhidhamma, Pali Text Society, 1969.

inasmuch as each of these elements is pleasant, beset with pleasure, immersed in pleasure, not in pain, therefore it is that beings get lusting after them.

If this earth-element, monks, this water-element, this heat-element, this air-element were entirely pleasant, beset with pleasure, immersed in pleasure, not immersed in pain, beings would not be repelled by them. But inasmuch as each of these elements is painful, is beset with pain, immersed in pain, not immersed in pleasure, therefore it is that beings are repelled by them."

We are bound to be attached to the elements when we buy beautiful clothes or enjoy delicious food. We are bound to be repelled by the elements when we get hurt or when we are sick. But no matter whether the objects we experience are pleasant or unpleasant, we should realize them as elements that arise because of their own conditions and that do not belong to us.

Questions

1. Is there nutrition with matter we call a table?

2. Why are eight rūpas called the "inseparable rūpas"?

3. Nutrition is one of the four factors which can produce rūpa. Can it produce the materiality we call "tree"?

Chapter 3

The Sense-Organs (Pasāda Rūpas)

So long as there are conditions for birth we have to be born and to experience pleasant or unpleasant objects. It is kamma that produces rebirth-consciousness as well as seeing, hearing and the other sense-impressions arising throughout our life. For the experience of objects through the senses there have to be sense-organs and these are rūpas produced by kamma as well. The sense-organs (pasāda rūpas) are physical results of kamma, whereas seeing, hearing and the other sense-impressions are nāma, vipākacittas which are the mental results of kamma[1].

Visible object and also the rūpa which is eyesense are conditions for seeing. Eyesense does not know anything since it is rūpa, but it is a necessary condition for seeing. Eyesense is a rūpa in the eye, capable of receiving visible object, so that citta can experience it. For hearing, the experience of sound, there has to be earsense, a rūpa in the ear, capable of receiving sound. There must be smellingsense for the experience of odour, tastingsense for the experience of flavour and bodysense for the experience of tangible object. Thus, there are five kinds of sense-organs.

As regards the eye, the "Atthasālinī" (II, Book II, Ch III, 306) distinguishes between the eye as "compound organ" and as "sentient

---
[1] See Introduction

organ", namely the rūpa which is eyesense, situated in the eye [2]. The eye as "compound organ" is described as follows:

> "... a lump of flesh is situated in the cavity of the eye, bound by the bone of the cavity of the eye below, by the bone of the brow above, by the eye-peaks on both sides, by the brain inside, by the eyelashes outside... Although the world perceives the eye as white, as (of a certain) bigness, extension, width, they do not know the real sentient eye, but only the physical basis thereof. That lump of flesh situated in the cavity of the eye is bound to the brain by sinewy threads. Therein are white, black, red, extension, cohesion, heat and mobility. The eye is white from the abundance of phlegm, black from that of bile, red from that of blood, rigid from the element of extension, fluid from that of cohesion, hot from that of heat, and oscillating from that of mobility. Such is the compound organ of the eye..."

As to the "sentient eye" or eyesense, this is to be found, according to the "Atthasālinī", in the middle of the black circle, surrounded by white circles, and it permeates the ocular membranes "as sprinkled oil permeates seven cotton wicks." We read:

> "And it is served by the four elements doing the functions of sustaining, binding, maturing and vibrating[3], just as a princely boy is tended by four nurses doing the functions of holding, bathing, dressing and fanning him. And being upheld by the caloric order, by thought (citta) and nutriment, and guarded by life and attended by colour, odour, taste, etc., the organ, no bigger in size than the head of a louse, stands duly fulfilling the nature of the basis and the door of visual cognition, etc. ..."

---

[2]In Pāli: cakkhu pasāda rūpa

[3]The earth element performs its function of sustaining, the water element of holding together, the fire element of maintaining or maturing, and the wind element of oscillation.

The "Visuddhimagga" (XIV, 37) gives the following definition of eye-sense[4]:

> "Herein, the eye's characteristic is sensitivity of primary elements that is ready for the impact of visible data; or its characteristic is sensitivity of primary elements originated by kamma sourcing from desire to see. Its function is to pick up (an object) among visible data. It is manifested as the footing of eye-consciousness. Its proximate cause is primary elements (the four Great Elements) born of kamma sourcing from desire to see."

We have desire to see, we are attached to all sense-impressions and, thus, there are still conditions for kamma to produce rebirth, to produce seeing, hearing and the other sense-impressions, and also to produce the sense-organs which are the conditions for the experience of sense objects. Also in future lives there are bound to be sense-impressions.

Eyesense seems to last and we are inclined to take it for "self". It seems that the same eyesense keeps on performing its function as a condition for seeing which also seems to last. However, eyesense arises and then falls away. At the next moment of seeing another eyesense has arisen. All these eyesenses are produced by kamma, throughout our life. We may find it hard to grasp this truth because we are so used to thinking of "my eyesense" and to consider it as something lasting.

The eyesense is extremely small, "no bigger in size than the head of a louse", but it seems that the whole wide world comes to us through the eye. All that is visible is experienced through the eye-sense, but when we believe that we see the world, there is thinking of a concept, not the experience of visible object. Our thinking is conditioned by seeing and by all the other sense-impressions.

The eye is compared to an ocean[5], because it cannot be filled, it is unsatiable. We are attached to the eyesense and we want to go on seeing, it never is enough.

---

[4]See also Dhammasangaṇi §597 and Atthasālinī II, Book II, Part I, Ch III, 312.
[5]Dhammasangaṇi §597. Atthasālinī II, Book II, Part I, Ch III, 308.

We read in the "Kindred Sayings" (IV, Saḷāyatana-vagga, Fourth Fifty, Ch 3, §187, The Ocean)[6]:

> "... The eye, bhikkhus, is the ocean for a person; its current consists of forms. One who withstands that current consisting of forms is said to have crossed the ocean of the eye with its waves, whirlpools, sharks and demons. Crossed over, gone beyond, the brahmin stands on high ground."

The same is said with regard to the other senses.

We read in the "Therī gāthā" (Psalms of the Sisters, Canto XIV, 71, Subhā of Jīvaka's Mango-grove) that the Therī Subhā became an anāgāmī[7]; she had eradicated clinging to sense objects. A young man, infatuated with the beauty of her eyes, wanted to tempt her. She warned him not to be deluded by the outward appearance of things. In reality there are only elements devoid of self. The Therī said about her eye (vs. 395):

> "What is this eye but a little ball lodged in the fork of a hollow tree,
>
> Bubble of film, anointed with tear-brine, exuding slime-drops.
>
> Compost wrought in the shape of an eye of manyfold aspects?..."

The Therī extracted one of her eyes and handed it to him. The impact of her lesson did not fail to cure the young man of his lust. Later on, in the presence of the Buddha, her eye was restored to her. She continued to develop insight and attained arahatship.

Eyesense is only an element devoid of self. It is one of the conditions for seeing. The "Visuddhimagga" (XV, 39) states about the

---

[6] I used the translation by Ven. Bodhi, "The Connected Discourses of the Buddha". "Form" is his translation of rūpa, which is actually visible object.

[7] There are four stages of enlightenment. The anāgāmī or "non-returner" has reached the third stage. The arahat has reached the last stage.

conditions for seeing: "Eye-consciousness arises due to eye, visible object, light and attention".

Earsense is another sense-organ. The "Atthasālinī" states that it is situated in the interior of the ear, "at a spot shaped like a finger-ring and fringed by tender, tawny hairs..." [8] Earsense is the rūpa which has the capability to receive sound. It is basis and door of hearing-consciousness. The "Visuddhimagga" (XIV, 38) gives the following definition[9]:

> "The ear's characteristic is sensitivity of primary elements that is ready for impact of sounds; or its characteristic is sensitivity of primary elements originated by kamma sourcing from desire to hear. Its function is to pick up (an object) among sounds. It is manifested as the footing of ear-consciousness. Its proximate cause is primary elements born of kamma sourcing from desire to hear."

Without earsense there cannot be hearing. The "Visuddhimagga" (XV, 39) states: "Ear-consciousness arises due to ear, sound, aperture and attention." "Aperture" is the cavity of the ear. If one of these conditions is lacking hearing cannot arise.

As to the other pasāda rūpas, smellingsense, tastingsense and bodysense, these are defined in the same way[10]. Smellingsense is a rūpa situated in the nose. It is one of the conditions for smelling. The "Visuddhimagga"(XV, 39) states: "Nose-consciousness arises due to nose, odour, air (the element of wind or motion) and attention." As to the element of wind or motion being a condition, we read in the "Atthasālinī" (II, Book II, Part I, Ch III, 315):

> "... the nose desires space, and has for object odour dependent on wind. Indeed, cattle at the first showers of rain keep smelling at the earth, and turning up their

---

[8] Atthasālinī II, Book II, Part I, Ch III, 310.
[9] See also "Dhammasangaṇi §601 and Atthasālinī II, Book II, Part I, Ch III, 312.
[10] See Dhammasangaṇi §605, 609, 613, Visuddhimagga XIV, 39, 40, 41, Atthasālinī, Book II, Part I, Ch III, 312.

muzzles to the sky breathe in the wind. And when a
fragrant lump is taken in the fingers and smelt, no smell
is got when breath is not inhaled..."

As to tastingsense, this is situated in the tongue and it is one of
the conditions for tasting. The "Visuddhimagga" states in the same
section: "Tongue-consciousness arises due to tongue, flavour, water
and attention." Also the element of water or cohesion plays its part
when tasting occurs. We read in the "Atthasālinī" (same section, 315)
about the element of water being a condition for tasting:

"... Thus even when a bhikkhu's duties have been done
during the three watches of the night, and he, early in
the morning, taking bowl and robe, has to enter the
village, he is not able to discern the taste of dry food if it
is unwetted by the saliva..."

As to bodysense, this is situated all over the body and inside
it, except in the hairs or tips of the nails. It is one of the conditions for experiencing tactile object. The "Visuddhimagga" states, in
the same section: "Body-consciousness arises due to body, tangible
object, earth and attention." The "Atthasālinī" (same section, 315)
explains:

"... Internal and external extension (solidity) is the cause
of the tactile sense seizing the object. Thus it is not
possible to know the hardness or softness of a bed well
spread out or of fruits placed in the hand, without
sitting down on the one or pressing the other. Hence
internal and external extension is the cause in the tactile
cognition of the tactile organ."

Thus, when tactile cognition, bodyconsciousness, arises, there are
actually elements impinging on elements. The impact of tactile object on the bodysense is more vigorous than the impact of the objects
on the other senses. According to the "Paramattha Mañjūsa", a commentary to the "Visuddhimagga"[11], because of the violence of the

---

[11]See Visuddhimagga, XIV, footnote 56.

impact on the bodysense, body-consciousness (kāyaviññāṇa) is accompanied either by pleasant feeling or by painful feeling, not by indifferent feeling, whereas the other sense-cognitions (seeing, hearing, etc.) are accompanied only by indifferent feeling.

Through the bodysense are experienced: the earth element, appearing as hardness or softness; the fire element, appearing as heat or cold; the wind element, appearing as motion or pressure. When these characteristics appear they can be directly experienced wherever there is bodysense, thus also inside the body.

As we have seen, visible object, sound, odour, flavour and tangible object (which consists of three of the four Great Elements) are experienced through the corresponding sense-doors and they can also be experienced through the mind-door. The sense-organs themselves through which the sense-objects are experienced are rūpas that can only be known through the mind-door.

The five sense-organs are the bases (vatthus) or places of origin of the corresponding sense-cognitions. Cittas do not arise outside the body, they are dependent on the physical bases where they originate [12]. The eyesense is the base where seeing-consciousness originates. The earsense is the base where hearing-consciousness originates, and it is the same in the case of the other sense-organs. As regards the base for body-consciousness, this can be at any place on the body where there is sensitivity. The sense-organs are bases only for the corresponding sense-cognitions. All the other cittas have another base, the heart-base; I shall deal with that later on.

The five sense-organs function also as doorways for the five kinds of sense-cognitions, as we have seen. The doorway (dvāra) is the means by which citta experiences an object. The eyesense is the doorway by which seeing-consciousness and also the other cittas arising in that process experience visible object. As we have seen, cittas which experience objects impinging on the senses and the mind-door time and again, arise in processes of cittas.[13] The cittas other than seeing-consciousness which arise in the eye-door process do

---

[12]There are also planes of existence where there is only nāma, not rūpa. In such planes cittas do not need a physical base.

[13]See Introduction.

not see, but they each perform their own function while they cognize visible object, such as considering visible object or investigating it. Each of the five sense-organs can be the doorway for all the cittas in the process experiencing a sense-object through that doorway. The sense-organs can have the function of base as well as doorway only in the case of the five sense-cognitions.

The sense-organs arise and fall away all the time and they are only doorway when an object is experienced through that sense-organ. Eyesense, for example, is only eye-door when visible object is experienced by the cittas arising in the eye-door process. When sound is experienced, earsense is doorway and eyesense does not function as doorway.

The "Atthasālinī" (II, Book II, Ch III, 316) states that "the senses are not mixed." They each have their own characteristic, function, manifestation and proximate cause, and through each of them the appropriate object is experienced. The earsense can only receive sound, not visible object or flavour. Hearing can only experience sound through the ear-door. We are not used to considering each doorway separately since we are inclined to think of a person who coordinates all experiences. We are inclined to forget that a citta arises because of conditions, experiences one object just for a moment, and then falls away immediately. In order to help people to have right understanding of realities, the Buddha spoke time and again about each of the six doorways separately. He told people to "guard" the doorways in being mindful, because on account of what is experienced through these doorways many kinds of defilements tend to arise.

We read in the "Kindred Sayings" (IV, Saḷāyatanavagga, Third Fifty, Ch 3, §127, Bhāradvāja) that King Udena asked the venerable Bhāradvāja what the cause was that young monks could practise the righteous life in its fulness and perfection. Bhāradvāja spoke about the advice the Buddha gave to them, such as seeing the foulness of the body, and guarding the six doors. We read that Bhāradvāja said:

> "... It has been said, Mahārājah, by the Exalted One...:
> 'Come, monks, do you abide watchful over the doors of

the faculties. Seeing an object with the eye, be not
misled by its outer view, nor by its lesser details. But
since coveting and dejection, evil, unprofitable states,
might overwhelm one who dwells with the faculty of the
eye uncontrolled, do you apply yourselves to such
control, set a guard over the faculty of the eye and attain
control of it. Hearing a sound with the ear... with the
nose smelling a scent... with the tongue tasting a
savour... with the body contacting tangibles... with the
mind cognizing mind-states... be you not misled by
their outward appearance nor by their lesser
details... attain control thereof...' "

We then read that King Udena praised the Buddha's words. He said about his own experiences:

"I myself, master Bhāradvāja, whenever I enter my
palace with body, speech and mind unguarded, with
thought unsettled, with my faculties uncontrolled, at
such times lustful states overwhelm me. But whenever,
master Bhāradvāja, I do so with body, speech and mind
guarded, with thought settled, with my faculties
controlled, at such times lustful states do not overwhelm
me..."

We read that King Udena took his refuge in the Buddha, the Dhamma and the Sangha. How can we avoid being misled by the outward appearance or by the details of phenomena? By understanding realities as they are when they appear, one at a time. The following sutta in the "Kindred Sayings"(IV, Saḷāyatanavagga, Second Fifty, Ch 3, §82, The World) reminds us not to cling to a "whole" but to be mindful of only one object at a time as it appears through one of the six doors:

"Then a certain monk came to see the Exalted
One... Seated at one side that monk said to the Exalted
One: 'The world! The world! is the saying, lord. How
far, lord, does this saying go?'

'It crumbles away, monks. Therefore it is called the world' [14]. What crumbles away? The eye ...objects...eye-consciousness...eye-contact...that pleasant or unpleasant or neutral feeling that arises owing to eye-contact ...tongue ...body ...mind ...It crumbles away, monks. Therefore it is called the world'."

Questions

1. Can eyesense experience something?

2. Where is the bodysense?

3. Is eyesense all the time eye-door?

4. For which type of citta is eyesense eye-door as well as base (vatthu, physical place of origin)?

---

[14] In Pāli there is a word association of loko, world, with lujjati, to crumble away.

Chapter 4

Sense Objects

We are infatuated with all the objects which are experienced through the sense-doors. However, they are only rūpas that fall away immediately; we cannot possess them. Sometimes we experience pleasant objects and sometimes unpleasant objects. The experience of a pleasant object is the result of kusala kamma and the experience of an unpleasant object is the result of akusala kamma.

The objects which can be experienced through the sense-doors are the following:

colour or visible object

sound

odour

flavour

tangible object

As we have seen in Chapter 2, three of the four Great Elements can be tangible object, namely: solidity (appearing as hardness or softness), temperature (appearing as heat or cold) and motion (appearing as motion, oscillation or pressure). The element of cohesion is not tangible object, it can be experienced only through the mind-door.

The sense objects which are visible object, odour and flavour are included in the "eight inseparable rūpas" which always arise together. As we have seen, rūpas arise in groups and with each group there have to be the eight inseparable rūpas which are the four Great Elements, visible object, odour, flavour and nutritive essence. Although these rūpas arise together, only one kind of rūpa at a time can be the object that is experienced. When there are conditions for the experience, for example, of flavour, the flavour that impinges on the tastingsense is experienced by tasting-consciousness. Flavour arises together with the other seven inseparable rūpas but these are not experienced at that moment.

Sound is the object of hearing-consciousness. Sound is not included in the eight inseparable rūpas, but when it arises it has to be accompanied by these rūpas that each perform their own function. Whenever sound occurs, there also have to be solidity, cohesion, temperature, motion and the other four inseparable rūpas. When sound is heard, the accompanying rūpas cannot be experienced. [1]

We read in the "Dhammasangaṇi" (§621) about different kinds of sounds, such as sound of drums and other musical instruments, sound of singing, noise of people, sound of substance against substance, sound of wind or water, human sound, such as sound of people talking. The "Atthasālinī" (II, Book II, Part I, Ch III, 319), which gives a further explanation of these kinds of sounds, defines sound as follows[2]:

> ... all sounds have the characteristic of striking the ear, the function and property of being the object of auditory cognition, the manifestation of being the field or object of auditory cognition...

Like the other sense objects, sound has as its proximate cause the four Great Elements. No matter what sound we hear, it has a

---

[1] Because each citta can experience only one object at a time through the appropriate doorway.
[2] See also Visuddhimagga XIV, 55.

degree of loudness and it "strikes the ear". Its characteristic can be experienced without the need to think about it. We may hear the sound of a bird and it seems that we know at once the origin of the sound. When we know the origin of the sound it is not hearing, but thinking of a concept. However, the thinking is conditioned by the hearing.

It seems that we can hear different sounds at a time, for example when a chord is played on the piano. When we recognize the different notes of a chord it is not hearing but thinking. When awareness arises, one reality at a time can be known as it is.

Sound can be produced by temperature or by citta. Sound of wind or sound of water is produced by temperature. Speech sound is produced by citta.

We are inclined to find a loud noise disturbing and we may make ourselves believe that at such a moment mindfulness of realities cannot arise. We read in the "Theragāthā" (Psalms of the Brothers, Part VII, Canto 62, Vajjiputta) about a monk of the Vajjian clan who was dwelling in a wood near Vesālī. The commentary to this verse (Paramatthadīpanī) states:

> "... Now a festival took place at Vesālī, and there was dancing, singing and reciting, all the people happily enjoying the festival. And the sound thereof distracted the bhikkhu, so that he quitted his solitude, gave up his exercise, and showed forth his disgust in this verse:
>
> Each by himself we in the forest dwell,
>
> Like logs rejected by the woodman's craft.
>
> So flit the days one like another by,
>
> Who more unlucky in their lot than we?
>
> Now a woodland deva heard him, and had compassion for the bhikkhu, and thus upbraided him, 'Even though you, bhikkhu, speak scornfully of forest life, the wise desiring solitude think much of it,' and to show him the advantage of it spoke this verse:

> Each by himself we in the forest dwell,
>
> Like logs rejected by the woodman's craft.
>
> And many a one does envy me my lot,
>
> Even as the hell-bound envies him who fares to heaven.
>
> Then the bhikkhu, stirred like a thoroughbred horse by the spur, went down into the avenue of insight, and striving soon won arahatship. Thereupon he thought, 'The deva's verse has been my goad!' and he recited it himself."

By this Sutta we are reminded that aversion to noise is not helpful. Mindfulness can arise of whatever reality presents itself. When sound appears, correct understanding of this reality can be developed. It can be known as a kind of rūpa and it does not matter what kind of sound it is. We are infatuated with pleasant sense objects and disturbed by unpleasant ones. Like and dislike are realities of daily life and they can be objects of awareness. We often find reasons why we cannot be mindful of the reality appearing at the present moment.

We would like to hear only pleasant things. When someone speaks unpleasant words to us we are inclined to think about this for a long time instead of being mindful of realities. We may forget that the moment of hearing is vipākacitta, result produced by kamma. Nobody can change vipāka. Hearing falls away immediately. When we think with aversion about the meaning of the words that were spoken, we accumulate unwholesomeness.

We read in the "Greater Discourse of the Elephant's Footprint" (Middle Length Sayings I, 28) that Sāriputta spoke to the monks about the elements that are conditioned, impermanent and devoid of self. He also spoke about the hearing of unpleasant words:

> " ... Your reverences, if others abuse, revile, annoy, vex this monk, he comprehends: 'This painful feeling that has arisen in me is born of sensory impingement on the ear, it has a cause, not no cause. What is the cause?

Sensory impingement is the cause.' He sees that sensory impingement is impermanent, he sees that feeling ... perception ... the habitual tendencies (saṅkhārakkhandha) are impermanent, he sees that consciousness is impermanent [3]. His mind rejoices, is pleased, composed, and is set on the objects of the element. If, your reverences, others comport themselves in undesirable, disagreeable, unpleasant ways towards that monk, and he receives blows from their hands and from clods of earth and from sticks and weapons, he comprehends thus: 'This body is such that blows from hands affect it and blows from clods of earth affect it and blows from sticks affect it and blows from weapons affect it. But this was said by the Lord in the Parable of the Saw: If, monks, low-down thieves should carve you limb from limb with a two-handled saw, whoever sets his heart at enmity, he, for this reason, is not a doer of my teaching. Unsluggish energy shall come to be stirred up by me, unmuddled mindfulness set up, the body tranquillised, impassible, the mind composed and onepointed. Now, willingly, let blows from hands affect this body, let blows from clods of earth ... from sticks ... from weapons affect it, for this teaching of the Awakened Ones is being done.' "

Do we see our experiences as elements to such a degree already that, when we hear unpleasant words, we can immediately realize: "This painful feeling that has arisen in me is born of sensory impingement on the ear"? In order to see realities as they are it is necessary to develop understanding of nāma and rūpa.

---

[3] This sutta refers to the five khandhas. Conditioned nāmas and rūpas can be classified as five khandhas or aggregates: rūpakkhandha (comprising all rūpas), vedanākkhandha or the khandha of feelings, saññākkhandha, the khandha of perception or remembrance, saṅkhārakkhandha, the khandha of "habitual tendencies" or "formations", including all cetasikas other than feeling and perception, viññāṇakkhandha, including all cittas.

There are different ways of classifying rūpas. One way is the classification as the four Great Elements (mahā-bhūta rūpas) and the derived rūpas (upāda rūpas), which are the other twentyfour rūpas among the twentyeight rūpas.

Another way is the classification as gross rūpas (oḷārika rūpas) and subtle rūpas (sukhuma rūpas). Twelve kinds of rūpa are gross; they are the sense-objects that can be experienced through the sense-doors, namely: visible object, sound, odour, flavour and the three rūpas that are tangible object, namely: solidity, temperature and motion, thus, three of the great Elements, and also the five sense-organs (pasāda rūpas) that can be the doors through which these objects are experienced. The other sixteen rūpas among the twentyeight kinds are subtle rūpas.

The "Visuddhimagga" (XIV, 73) states that twelve rūpas "are to be taken as gross because of impinging; the rest is subtle because they are the opposite of that." The seven rūpas that can be sense objects[4] are impinging time and again on the five rūpas which are the sense organs. Subtle rūpas do not impinge on the senses. According to the "Visuddhimagga", the subtle rūpas are far, because they are difficult to penetrate, whereas the gross rūpas are near, because they are easy to penetrate.

Objects impinge on the senses time and again, but we are usually forgetful of realities. We have learnt about the four Great Elements and other rūpas and we may begin to notice different characteristics of realities when they present themselves. For example, when we are walking, rūpas such as hardness, heat or pressure may appear one at a time. We can learn the difference between the moments when characteristics of realities appear one at a time and when we are thinking of concepts such as feet and ground. The ground cannot impinge on the bodysense and be directly experienced. The Buddha urged the monks to develop right understanding during all their actions. We read in the commentary to the "Satipaṭṭhāna Sutta"[5], in

---

[4]They are visible object, sound, odour, flavour and three tangible objects which are three among the Great Elements.

[5]In the Middle Length Sayings I, no 10. See the translation of the commentary to this sutta in "The Way of Mindfulness" by Ven. Soma, B.P.S. Kandy, 1975.

the section on the four kinds of Clear Comprehension, about clear comprehension in wearing robes:

> " ... Within there is nothing called a soul that robes itself. According to the method of exposition adopted already, only, by the diffusion of the process of oscillation (the element of wind or motion) born of mental activity does the act of robing take place. The robe has no power to think and the body too has not that power. The robe is not aware of the fact that it is draping the body, and the body too of itself does not think: 'I am being draped round with the robe.' Mere processes clothe a process-heap, in the same way that a modelled figure is covered with a piece of cloth. Therefore, there is neither room for elation on getting a fine robe nor for depression on getting one that is not fine."

This passage is a good reminder of the truth, also for laypeople. We are used to the impact of clothes on the body, most of the time we do not even notice it. Or we are taken in by the pleasantness of soft material that touches the body, or by the colour of our clothes. We can be mindful of softness or colour as only elements. In reality there are only elements impinging on elements.

We read in the "Gradual Sayings" (II, Book of the Fours, Ch XVIII, §7, Rāhula) that the Buddha said to Rāhula:

> "Rāhula, what is the inward earth-element and what is the external earth-element, these are just this earth-element. Thus it should be regarded, as it really is, by perfect wisdom: 'This is not of me. Not this am I. Not to me is this the self.' So seeing it, as it really is, by perfect wisdom, one has revulsion for the earth-element; by wisdom one cleanses the heart of passion."

The same is said of the elements of water, heat and wind. The Buddha then said:

"Now, Rāhula, when a monk beholds neither the self nor what pertains to the self in these four elements, this one is called 'a monk who has cut off craving, has loosed the bond, and by perfectly understanding (this) vain conceit, has made an end of Ill.'"

Questions

1. Which factors can produce sound?
2. When someone speaks, by which factor is sound produced?
3. Why are gross rūpas so called?
4. Which rūpas among the inseparable rūpas are gross?
5. Through which doorways can gross rūpas be known?

Chapter 5

Subtle Rūpas produced by Kamma

The objects that can be experienced through the sense-doors as well as the sense-organs themselves are gross rūpas, the other rūpas are subtle rūpas. As we have seen, seven rūpas are sense objects, namely, colour or visible object, sound, odour, flavour and tangible object including three of the four Great Elements which are solidity, temperature and motion. Five rūpas are sense-organs, namely, eyesense, earsense, nosesense, tonguesense and bodysense. The sense objects impinge on the relevant senses so that seeing, hearing and the other sense-cognitions can arise time and again in daily life.

Among the twentyeight kinds of rūpas, the sense objects and the sense-organs are twelve rūpas which are gross, whereas the other sixteen rūpas are subtle rūpas.

The sense-organs are produced solely by kamma, not by the other three factors of citta, temperature and nutrition which can produce rūpas. There are also subtle rūpas which are produced solely by kamma. They are: the femininity-faculty, the masculinity-faculty, the life-faculty and the heart-base.

With regard to the femininity-faculty (itthindriyaṃ) and the masculinity-faculty (purisindriyaṃ), collectively called bhāvarūpa or sex, these are rūpas produced by kamma from the first moment of our life and throughout life. Thus, it is due to kamma whether one is born as a male or as a female. The "Atthasālinī" (II, Book II, Part I,

Ch III, 322) explains that birth as a male and birth as a female are different kinds of vipāka. Being born as a human being is kusala vipāka, but since good deeds have different degrees also their results have different degrees. Birth as a female is the result of kusala kamma of a lesser degree than the kusala kamma that conditions birth as a male. In the course of life one can notice the difference between the status of men and that of women. It is a fact that in society generally men are esteemed higher than women. Usually women cannot so easily obtain a position of honour in society. But as regards the development of wisdom, both men and women can develop it and attain arahatship. We read in the "Kindred Sayings" (IV, Saḷāyatana-vagga, Part III, Kindred Sayings about Womankind, 3, §34, Growth):

> "Increasing in five growths, monks, the ariyan woman disciple increases in the ariyan growth, takes hold of the essential, takes hold of the better. What five?
>
> She grows in confidence (saddhā), grows in virtue (sī la), in learning, in generosity, in wisdom. Making such growth, monks, she takes hold of the essential, she takes hold of the better ... "

The "Atthasālinī" (II, Book II, Ch III, 321) explains that women and men have different features, that they are different in outer appearance, in occupation and deportment. The feminine features, etc. are conditioned by the rūpa that is the femininity faculty. The "Atthasālinī" states about these features:

> " ... They are produced in course of process because of that faculty. When there is seed the tree grows because of the seed, and is replete with branch and twig and stands filling the sky; so when there is the feminine controlling faculty called femininity, feminine features, etc. , come to be ... "

The same is said about the masculinity faculty. Femininity and masculinity are "controlling faculties". A controlling faculty or indriya is a "leader" in its own field, it has a predominant influence.

The controlling faculties of femininity and masculinity permeate the whole body so that they are manifested in the outward appearance and features of a woman and a man.

The "Atthasālinī" (same section, 322) gives the following definitions of the femininity faculty and the masculinity faculty:

> "Of these two controlling faculties the feminine has the characteristic of (knowing) the state of woman, the function of showing "this is woman", the manifestation which is the cause of femininity in feature, mark, occupation, deportment.
>
> The masculinity controlling faculty has the characteristic of (knowing) the state of man, the function of showing "this is man", the manifestation which is the cause of masculinity in feature, etc. [1]"

These two faculties which, as the Visuddhimagga (XIV, 58) explains, are "coextensive with" or pervade the whole body, are not known by visual cognition but only by mind-cognition. But, as the "Atthasālinī" (321) states, their characteristic features, etc., which are conditioned by their respective faculties, can be known by visual cognition as well as by mind-cognition.

Seeing experiences only visible object, it does not know "This is a woman" or "This is a man". The citta which recognizes feminine or masculine features does so through the mind-door, but this recognizing is conditioned by seeing. When the commentary states that these characteristic features are known by visual cognition as well as by mind-cognition, it does not speak in detail about the different processes of cittas experiencing objects through the eye-door and through the mind-door.

Generally, women like to emphasize their femininity in make up and clothes and also men like to emphasize their masculinity in their outward appearance and behaviour. One clings to one's feminine or masculine features, one's way of deportment. We should not forget that it is the femininity faculty or masculinity faculty, only a rūpa

---

[1] See also Dhammasangaṇi §633, 634 and Visuddhimagga XIV, 58.

produced by kamma, which conditions our outward appearance or deportment to be specifically feminine or masculine. We take our sex for self, but it is only a conditioned element devoid of self.

Life faculty, the rūpa which is jīvitindriya, is also a subtle rūpa produced by kamma from the first moment of life and throughout life.

Apart from rūpa-jīvitindriya there is also nāma-jīvitindriya. Nāma-jīvitindriya is a cetasika among the "universals", cetasikas which accompany every citta. This cetasika supports the citta and the cetasikas it arises together with, it maintains their life.

The rūpa that is life faculty, rūpa-jīvitindriya, sustains and maintains the rūpas it accompanies in one group of rūpas. This kind of rūpa is produced solely by kamma, it arises only in living beings. Therefore, the rūpas in the bodies of living beings are different from those in dead matter or plants which are produced solely by temperature or the element of heat. The rūpa that is life faculty is contained in each group of rūpas of the body produced by kamma.

Life faculty is a "controlling faculty" (indriya), it has a dominating influence over the other rūpas it arises together with since it maintains their life. The "Visuddhimagga" (XIV, 59) states about life faculty:[2]

> "The life faculty has the characteristic of maintaining conascent kinds of matter.[3] Its function is to make them occur. It is manifested in the establishing of their presence. Its proximate cause is primary elements that are to be sustained."

Life faculty maintains the other rūpas it arises together with in one group, and then it falls away together with them. The "Visuddhimagga" (in the same section) states:

> "It does not prolong presence at the moment of dissolution because it is itself dissolving, like the flame

---

[2] See also Dhammasangaṇi §635. The Atthasālinī refers to its definition of nāma-jīvitindriya (I, Part IV, Ch I, 123, 124)

[3] The rūpas arising together with it.

of a lamp when the wick and the oil are getting used up..."

We cling to our body as something alive. Rūpas of a "living body" have a quality lacking in dead matter or plants, they are supported by the life faculty. We are inclined to take this quality for "self", but it is only a rūpa produced by kamma.

The heart-base (hadayavatthu) is another rūpa produced solely by kamma. In the planes of existence where there are nāma and rūpa, cittas have a physical place of origin, a base (vatthu). Seeing-consciousness has as its base the eye-base, the rūpa which is eye-sense, and evenso have the other sense-cognitions their appropriate bases where they arise. Apart from the sense-bases there is another base: the heart-base. This is the place of origin for all cittas other than the sense-cognitions.

At the first moment of life the rebirth-consciousness (patisandhi-citta) which arises is produced by kamma. If this citta arises in a plane of existence where there are nāma and rūpa it must have a physical base: this is the heart-base, which is produced by kamma. Kamma produces this rūpa from the first moment of life and throughout life.

The rūpa which is the heart-base has not been classified as such in the "Dhammasangaṇi", but it is referred to as "this rūpa" in the "Book of Conditional Relations" (Paṭṭhāna), the Seventh Book of the Abhidhamma. In the section on "Dependance Condition" (Part II, Analytical Exposition of Conditions) it is said that dependant on the five sense-bases the five sense-cognitions arise and that dependant on "this matter" mind-element and mind-consciousness-element arise. "This matter" is the rūpa which is the heart-base; the mind-element and mind-consciousness-element comprise all cittas other than the five sense-cognitions.[4] The sense-cognitions of seeing, etc. have the appropriate sense-base as physical base, and all other cittas have the heart-base as physical base.

---

[4]Mind-element are the five-sense-door adverting-consciousness and the two types of receiving-consciousness, which are kusala vipāka and akusala vipāka. Mind-consciousness-element are all cittas other than the sense-cognitions and mind-element.

The "Visuddhimagga" (XIV, 60) gives the following definition of the heart-base[5]:

> "The heart-basis has the characteristic of being the (material) support for the mind-element and for the mind-consciousness-element. Its function is to support them. It is manifested as the carrying of them ... "

The "Visuddhimagga" (VIII, 111,112) states that the heart-base is to be found inside the heart. It is of no use to speculate where exactly the heart-base is. It is sufficient to know that there is a rūpa which is base for all cittas other than the sense-cognitions. We may not experience the heart-base as such, but if there would be no heart-base we could not think at this moment, we could not know which objects we are experiencing, we could not feel happy or unhappy. In the planes of existence where there are nāma and rūpa all cittas must have a physical base, they cannot arise outside the body. When we, for example, are angry, cittas rooted in aversion arise and these originate at the heart-base.

If we had not studied the Abhidhamma we would have thought that all cittas originate in what we call in conventional language "brain". One may cling to a concept of brain and take it for self. The Abhidhamma can clear up misunderstandings about bodily phenomena and mental phenomena and the way they function. It explains how physical phenomena and mental phenomena are interrelated. Mental phenomena are dependant on physical phenomena[6] and physical phenomena can have mental phenomena as conditioning factors.

The conditioning factors for what we call body and mind are impermanent. Why then do we take body and mind for something permanent? We read in the "Kindred Sayings" (III, Khandhā-vagga,

---

[5]The Atthasālinī does not classify the heart-base separately, but it mentions the "basis-decad", a group of ten rūpas including the heart-base (Book II, Ch III, 316). As I shall explain later on, from the first moment of our life kamma produces three decads, groups of ten rūpas: the bodysense-decad, the sex-decad and the heart-base-decad.

[6]In the planes of existence where there are nāma and rūpa.

Kindred Sayings on Elements, First Fifty, Ch 2, §18, Cause) that the Buddha said to the monks at Sāvatthī:

> "Body, monks is impermanent. That which is the cause, that which is the condition for the arising of body, that also is impermanent. How, monks, can a body which is compounded of the impermanent come to be permanent? ..."

The same is said about the mental phenomena (classified as four aggregates or khandhas). We then read:

> "Thus seeing, the welltaught ariyan disciple[7] is repelled by body, is repelled by feeling, by perception, by the 'activities' [8]. He is repelled by consciousness. Being repelled by it he lusts not for it: not lusting he is set free. Thus he realizes: 'Rebirth is destroyed, lived is the righteous life, done is my task, for life in these conditions there is no here-after.' "

Questions

1. Why can life faculty not arise in plants?

2. What is the base for citta rooted in aversion?

3. Does the brain have the function of base for cittas?

4. What is the base for rebirth-consciousness in the human plane of existence?

---

[7] An ariyan is a person who has attained enlightenment.
[8] Cetasikas other than feeling and perception are classified as one khandha, that of the activities or formations, saṅkhārakkhandha.

Chapter 6

Intimation through Body and Speech

Citta is one of the four factors that produces rūpa. We look different when we laugh, when we cry, when we are angry or when we are generous. Then we can notice that citta produces rūpa.

Bodily intimation (kāyaviññatti) and speech intimation (vacī viññatti) are two kinds of rūpa, originated by citta. They are not produced by the other three factors that can produce rūpa, by kamma, temperature or nutrition.

As to bodily intimation, this is a specific way of expression by rūpas of the body that display our intentions, be they wholesome or unwholesome. Our intentions can be expressed by way of movement of the body, of the limbs, facial movement or gestures. The intention expressed through bodily intimation can be understood by others, even by animals. Bodily intimation itself is rūpa, it does not know anything. We read in the "Dhammasangaṇi" (§636):

> "What is that rūpa which is bodily intimation (kāyaviññatti)?
>
> That tension, that intentness, that state of making the body tense, in response to a thought, whether good or bad, or indeterminate (kiriyacitta), on the part of one who advances, or recedes, or fixes the gaze, or glances around, or retracts an arm, or stretches it forth - the

intimation, the making known, the state of having made known - this is that rūpa which constitutes bodily intimation."

Citta is one of the factors that produces groups of the "eight inseparable rūpas" of the body[1] and among them the element of wind or motion plays its specific part in causing motion of rūpas of the body so that intimation can be displayed.

The "Atthasālinī" (I, Book I, Part III, 82, 83) states about bodily intimation:

> "Because it is a capacity of communicating, it is called "intimation". What does it communicate? A certain wish communicable by an act of the body. If anyone stands in the path of the eye, raises his hands or feet, shakes his head or brow, the movement of his hands, etc. are visible. Intimation, however, is not so visible; it is only knowable by the mind. For one sees by the eye a colour-surface moving by virtue of the change of position in hands, etc.[2] But by reflecting on it as intimation, one knows it by mind-door-consciousness, thus: 'Imagine that this man wishes me to do this or that act.' ... "

The intention expressed through bodily intimation is intelligible to others, not through the eye-door but through the mind-door. Knowing, for example, that someone waves is cognition through the mind-door and this cognition is conditioned by seeing-consciousness that experiences visible object or colour. The meaning of what has been intimated is known by reflection on it, thus it can only be cognized through the mind-door.

The "Visuddhimagga" (XIV, 61) defines intimation in a similar way and then states about its function, manifestation and proximate cause:

---

[1] The four Great Elements of solidity, cohesion, temperature and motion, and visible object, odour, flavour and nutrition.

[2] Because of saññā, remembrance, one can perceive the movement of a colour surface. Seeing sees only colour, it cannot see movement of colour.

> "... Its function is to display intention. It is manifested as the cause of bodily excitement. Its proximate cause is the consciousness-originated air- element."

As to the proximate cause, as we have seen, the element of wind (air) or motion plays its specific role in the intimating of intention by bodily movement or gestures.

We are inclined to take intimation as belonging to self, but bodily intimation is only a kind of rūpa, originated by citta. There is no person who communicates by gestures. Are we aware of nāma and rūpa when we gesticulate? Are there kusala cittas or akusala cittas at such moments? Most of the time akusala cittas arise, but we do not notice it. Do we realize which type of citta conditions the bodily intimation when we wave to someone else in order to greet him, when we gesticulate in order to tell him to come nearer, when we nod our head while we agree with something or shake it while we deny something? Such gestures are part of our daily routine and it seems that we make them automatically. Perhaps we never considered what types of citta condition them. Akusala citta conditions bodily intimation, for example, when we with mimics ridicule someone else or show our contempt for him. In such cases it is obvious that there is akusala citta. We should remember that bodily intimation is more often conditioned by akusala citta than by kusala citta. There may be subtle clinging that is not so obvious while we are expressing our intention by gestures. When mindfulness arises we can find out whether kusala citta or akusala citta motivates our gestures. Someone may also commit akusala kamma through bodily intimation, for example when he gives by gesture orders to kill. Kusala cittas may condition bodily intimation when we, for example, stretch out our arms to welcome people to our home, when we stretch out our hand in order to give something, when we point out the way to someone who is in a strange city, when we by our gestures express courtesy or when we show respect to someone who deserves respect. However, we may also perform such actions because of selfish motives, or we may be insincere, and then akusala cittas condition bodily intimation. More knowledge about citta and rūpas which are conditioned by citta can remind us to be aware of whatever reality appears, also while gesticulating. Then akusala citta has no opportunity to arise at such moments.

Our intentions are not only communicated by gestures, but also by speech. Speech intimation (vacī viññatti) is a kind of rūpa, originated by citta. The "Dhammasangaṇi" (Ch II, §637) states:

> "What is that rūpa which is intimation by language (vacī viññatti)?
>
> That speech, voice, enunciation, utterance, noise, making noises, language as articulate speech, which expresses a thought whether good, bad, or indeterminate - this is called language. And that intimation, that making known, the state of having made known by language - this is that rūpa which constitutes intimation by language."

When someone's intention is intimated through speech, it is intelligible to others. The meaning of what is intimated is known by reflection about it, thus, it is cognizable through the mind-door. Speech intimation itself does not know anything, it is rūpa.

Citta is one of the factors that produces the "eight inseparable rūpas" of the body and among them the element of earth or hardness plays a specific part in the conditioning of speech intimation.

The "Visuddhimagga" (XIV, 62)[3] states that the function of speech intimation is to display intention, its manifestation is causing speech sound, and that its proximate cause is the earth element originated from citta. The proximate cause of bodily intimation is the element of wind or motion which is produced by citta, whereas the proximate cause of speech intimation is the element of earth or hardness which is produced by citta. When speech-intimation occurs it is the condition for the rūpas which are the means of articulation, such as rūpas of the lips, to produce speech sound.

Rūpas can be classified as sabhāva rūpas, rūpas with their own distinct nature (sa meaning: with, bhāva meaning: nature) and asabh-

---

[3] See Atthasālinī I, Book I, Part III, Ch 2, 86,87, and II, Book II, Part I, Ch 3, 324.

āva rūpas, rūpas without their own distinct nature. The eight inseparable rūpas are sabhāva rūpas, they each have their own distinct nature and characteristic. Bodily intimation and speech intimation are rūpas conditioned by citta, but these two kinds of rūpa are not rūpas with their own distinct nature and characteristic. They are, as the "Atthasālinī" expresses it, a "certain, unique change" in the great elements which are produced by citta and which are the condition for the two kinds of intimation. They are qualities of rūpa and therefore, asabhāva rūpas. The eight inseparable rūpas on which the two kinds of intimation depend are produced by citta, according to the "Atthasālinī" (II, Book II, Part I, Ch 3, 337).

Do we realize whether speech intimation is conditioned by kusala citta or by akusala citta? We may know in theory that we speak with akusala citta when our objective is not wholesomeness, such as generosity, kindness or the development of understanding of the Buddha's teachings, but do we realize this at the moments we speak? Even when akusala kamma through speech, such as lying or slandering, is not committed, we may still speak with akusala citta. We may find out that often our speech is motivated by akusala citta. We speak with cittas rooted in attachment when we want to gain something, when we want to be liked or admired by others. With this objective we may even tell "tales" about others, ridicule or denigrate them. We are attached to speech and we often chatter just in order to keep the conversation going. We tend to feel lonely when there is silence. Usually we do not consider whether what we say is beneficial or not. We have to speak to others when we organize our work in the office or at home. Do we realize whether there are at such moments kusala cittas or akusala cittas? When we lie we commit akusala kamma through speech.

Speech intimation is produced by kusala citta when we, for example, with generosity and kindness try to help and encourage others in speaking to them. When we speak about the Buddha's teachings there may be kusala cittas, but at times there also tend to be akusala cittas, for example, when we are conceited about our knowledge, or when we are attached to the people we are speaking to. Many different types of citta arise and fall away very rapidly and we may not know when the citta is kusala citta and when akusala citta. There can be mindfulness of nāma and rūpa while speaking. One may believe that this is not possible because one has to think of the words one wants to speak. However, thinking is a reality and it can also be object of mindfulness. There are sound and hearing and they can be object of mindfulness when they appear. We are usually absorbed in the subject we want to speak about and we attach great importance to our speech. We live most of the time in the world of "conventional truth", and we are forgetful of ultimate realities (paramattha dhammas). In the ultimate sense there is no speaker, only phenomena, devoid of self, conditioned nāmas and rūpas.

When we gesticulate and speak, hardness, pressure, sound or hearing may present themselves, they can be experienced one at a time. If there is mindfulness at such moments, understanding of the reality that appears can be developed.

The "Visuddhimagga" (XVIII, 31) uses a simile of a marionette in order to illustrate that there is no human being in the ultimate sense, only conditioned phenomena. We read:

> "Therefore, just as a marionette is void, soulless and without curiosity, and while it walks and stands merely through the combination of strings and wood, yet it seems as if it had curiosity and interestedness, so too, this mentality-materiality is void, soulless and without curiosity, and while it walks and stands merely through the combination of the two together, yet it seems as if it had curiosity and interestedness. This is how it should be regarded. Hence the Ancients said:
>
> 'The mental and material are really here,
>
> 'But here there is no human being to be found,
>
> 'For it is void and merely fashioned like a doll–
>
> 'Just suffering piled up like grass and sticks."

When one sees a performance with marionettes, it seems that the puppets have lives of their own: they exert themselves, they are absorbed, attached or full of hatred and sorrow, and one can laugh and cry because of the story that is being enacted. However, the puppets are only wood and strings, held by men who make them act. When one sees how the puppets are stored after the play they are not impressive anymore, only pieces of wood and strings. When we study the Abhidhamma it helps us to understand more that this marionette we call "self" can move about, act and speak because of the appropriate conditions.

As we have seen in the definitions of the two kinds of intimation by the 'Dhammasangaṇi" (§636, 637), these two kinds of rūpa can be conditioned by kusala citta, akusala citta or "inoperative" citta (kiriy-acitta). When we realize that intimation through body and speech is very often conditioned by akusala citta, we come to see the danger of being forgetful of nāma and rūpa while we make gestures and speak. Then we are urged to remember the Buddha's words as to the practice of "clear comprehension" (sampajañña) in the "Satipaṭṭhāna Sutta" (Middle Length Sayings no. 10, in the section on Mindfulness of the Body, dealing with the four kinds of clear comprehension[4]) :

> "And further, bhikkhus, a bhikkhu, in going forwards (and) in going backwards, is a person practising clear comprehension; in looking straight on (and) in looking away from the front, is a person practising clear comprehension; in bending and in stretching, is a person practising clear comprehension; in wearing the shoulder-cloak, the (other two) robes (and) the bowl, is a person practising clear comprehension; in regard to what is eaten, drunk, chewed and savoured, is a person practising clear comprehension; in defecating and in urinating, is a person practising clear comprehension; in walking, in standing (in a place), in sitting (in some position), in sleeping, in waking, in speaking and in keeping silence, is a person practising clear comprehension."

---
[4] See the translation in "The Way of Mindfulness" by Ven. Soma.

Questions

1. Can bodily intimation be the body-door through which a good deed or an evil deed is being performed?

2. Through which door can what is being intimated by bodily movement be recognized?

3. When a conductor conducts an orchestra and he makes gestures in order to show the musicians how to play the music, which types of citta can produce the bodily intimation?

4. When one slanders, which type of rūpa is the door through which such action is being performed?

5. When we speak to others in order to organize our work, can speech be conditioned by akusala citta?

Chapter 7

Rūpas from different Factors

The study of rūpas produced by kamma, citta, temperature or nutrition is beneficial for the understanding of our daily life. When we study the conditions for our daily experiences and bodily functions, we shall better understand that our life is only nāma and rūpa. This again reminds us to be aware so that realities can be known as they are.

In this human plane of existence experiences through the senses arise time and again, such as seeing and hearing, and these could not occur without the body. The sense-cognitions have as their physical places of origin their appropriate sense-bases (vatthus) and these are produced by kamma throughout our life. All other cittas have as their physical base the heart-base (hadaya-vatthu) and this kind of rūpa is produced by kamma from the first moment of life. In the planes of existence where there are nāma and rūpa, citta needs a physical base, it could not arise without the body. The rūpa that is life-faculty (jīvitindriya) is also produced by kamma from the first moment of life. It supports the other rūpas of the group of rūpas produced by kamma. Moreover, it is due to kamma whether we are born as a female or as a male. The rūpas that are the femininity-faculty (itthindriyaṃ) and the masculinity-faculty (purisindriyaṃ) have a great influence on our daily life. They condition our outward appearance, our behaviour, the way we walk, stand, sit or lie down, our voice, our occupation, our place and status in society. All these kinds of rūpa produced by kamma arise in groups, that always include the eight inseparable rūpas and also life-faculty.

Some kinds of rūpa are produced solely by kamma, some are produced solely by citta, such as bodily intimation (kaya-viññatti) and speech-intimation (vacī-viññatti). Some kinds of rūpa can be produced by kamma, citta, temperature or nutrition. The eight inseparable rūpas of solidity, cohesion, temperature, motion, colour, odour, flavour and nutrition can be produced by either one of the four factors. If kamma produces them, they always arise together with life-faculty, and in addition they can arise with other rūpas produced by kamma. Citta produces groups of the eight inseparable rūpas from the moment the bhavanga-citta (life-continuum) that succeeds the rebirth-consciousness arises.

The following three kinds of rūpa are sometimes produced by citta, sometimes by temperature, sometimes by nutrition. They are:

buoyancy or lightness (lahutā)

plasticity (mudutā)

wieldiness (kammaññatā)

ṅ
Because of lightness, our body is not heavy or sluggish. Because of plasticity it is pliable, it has elasticity and is not stiff. Because of wieldiness it has adaptability. For the movement of the body and the performance of its functions, these three qualities are essential. They arise in the bodies of living beings, not in dead matter. These three rūpas are rūpas without a distinct nature, asabhāva rūpas; they are qualities of rūpa, namely, changeability of rūpa (vikāra rūpas, vikāra meaning change)[1]. The "Atthasālinī" (II, Book II, Part I, Ch III, 326) gives the following definitions of these three kinds of rūpa [2] :

---

[1] As we have seen in Ch 6, the two rūpas of bodily intimation, kāya viññatti, and speech intimation, vāci viññatti, are also qualities of rūpa that are changeability of rūpa, vikāra rūpas. In some texts bodily intimation and speech intimation are classified separately as the two rūpas of intimation, viññatti rūpas.

[2] See also Dhammasangaṇi §639 - 641 and Visuddhimagga XIV, 64.

> "... buoyancy of matter has non-sluggishness as its characteristic, removing the heaviness of material objects as its function, quickness of change as its manifestation, buoyant matter as its proximate cause.
>
> Next 'plasticity of matter' has non-rigidity as characteristic, removing the rigidity of material objects as function, absence of opposition in all acts due to its own plasticity as manifestation, plastic matter as proximate cause.
>
> 'Wieldiness of matter' has workableness suitable or favorable to bodily actions as characteristic, removal of non-workableness as function, non- weakness as manifestation, workable matter as proximate cause."

The "Atthasālinī" also states that these three qualities "do not abandon each other". When one of them arises, the others have to arise as well. They never arise without the eight inseparable rūpas. Although the qualities of lightness, plasticity and wieldiness arise together, they are different from each other. The "Atthasālinī" (in the same section) explains their differences. Buoyancy is non-sluggishness and it is like the quick movement of one free from ailment. Plasticity is plasticity of objects like well-pounded leather, and it is distinguished by tractability. Wieldiness is wieldiness of objects like well-polished gold and it is distinguished by suitableness for all bodily actions. When one is sick, the elements of the body are disturbed, and the body is sluggish, stiff and without adaptability. We read in the "Visuddhimagga" (VIII, 28) about the disturbance of the elements:

> "... But with the disturbance of the earth element even a strong man's life can be terminated if his body becomes rigid, or with the disturbance of one of the elements beginning with water if his body becomes flaccid and putrifies with a flux of the bowels, etc., or if he is consumed by a bad fever, or if he suffers a severing of his limb-joint ligatures."

When one is healthy, there are conditions for lightness, plasticity and wieldiness of body. The "Atthasālinī" states that these three qualities are not produced by kamma, but that they are produced by citta, temperature or nutrition. This commentary states (in the same section, 327):

" ... Thus ascetics say, 'Today we have agreeable food ... today we have suitable weather ... today our mind is one-pointed, our body is light, plastic and wieldy.' "

When we have suitable food and the temperature is right we may notice that we are healthy, that the body is not rigid and that it can move in a supple way. Not only food and temperature, also kusala citta can influence our physical condition. When we apply ourselves to mental development it can condition suppleness of the body. Thus we can verify in our daily life what is taught in the Abhidhamma.

Lightness, plasticity and wieldiness condition our bodily movements to be supple. When we are speaking they condition the function of speech to be supple and "workable". Whenever we notice that there are bodily lightness, plasticity and wieldiness, we should remember that they are qualities of rūpa, conditioned by citta, temperature or nutrition.

Rūpas always arise in groups (kalapas) consisting of at least eight rūpas, the eight inseparable rūpas. There are rūpas other than these eight and these arise in a group together with the eight inseparable rūpas. Our body consists of different groups of rūpas and each group is surrounded by infinitesimally tiny space, and this is the rūpa that is called space (akāsa)[3]. The rūpas within a group are holding tightly together and cannot be divided, and the rūpa space allows the different groups to be distinct from each other. Thus, its function is separating or delimiting the different groups of rūpas, and therefore it is also called pariccheda rūpa, the rūpa that delimits (pariccheda meaning limit or boundary). The rūpa space is a rūpa without its own distinct nature (asabhāva rūpa), and it arises simultaneously with the different groups of rūpa it surrounds.

---

[3]I used for the description of space Acharn Sujin's "Survey of Paramattha Dhammas", Ch 4.

The "Atthasālinī" (II, Book II, Part I, Ch III, 326) states that space is that which cannot be scratched, cut or broken. It is "untouched by the four great Elements." Space cannot be touched. The "Atthasālinī" gives the following definition of space [4]:

> "... space-element has the characteristic of delimiting material objects, the function of showing their boundaries, the manifestation of showing their limits, state of being untouched by the four great elements and of being their holes and openings as manifestation, the separated objects as proximate cause. It is that of which in the separated groups we say 'this is above, this is below, this is across.'"

Space delimits the groups of rūpa that are produced by kamma, citta, temperature and nutrition so that they are separated from each other. If there were no space in between the different groups of rūpa, these groups would all be connected, not distinct from each other. Space comes into being as it surrounds the groups of rūpas produced by kamma, citta, temperature and nutrition and, thus, it is regarded as originating from each of these four factors.

We read in the "Discourse on the Analysis of the Elements" (Middle Length Sayings III, no 140) that the Buddha explained to the monk Pukkusāti about the elements and that he also spoke about the element of space. This Sutta refers to the empty space of holes and openings that are, as we have read, the manifestation of space. We read:

> "... And what, monk, is the element of space? The element of space may be internal, it may be external. And what, monk, is the internal element of space? Whatever is space, spacious, is internal, referable to an individual and derived therefrom, such as the auditory and nasal orifices, the door of the mouth and that by which one swallows what is munched, drunk, eaten and

---

[4] See also Dhammasangaṇi, §638 and Visuddhimagga XIV, 63.

tasted, and where this remains, and where it passes out (of the body) lower down, or whatever other thing is space, spacious, is internal, referable to an individual and derived therefrom, this, monk, is called the internal element of space. Whatever is an internal element of space and whatever is an external element of space, just these are the element of space. By means of perfect intuitive wisdom this should be seen as it really is thus: This is not mine, this am I not, this is not myself. Having seen this thus as it really is by means of perfect intuitive wisdom, he disregards the element of space, he cleanses his mind of the element of space."

The Sutta speaks about space of the auditory orifices and the other holes and openings of the body. Space in the ear is one of the conditions for hearing[5]. We attach great importance to internal space and we take it for "mine" or self, but it is only a rūpa element.

Questions

1. When we notice suppleness of the limbs, is this experienced through the bodysense?

2. Can suitable food, suitable weather and the citta which, for example, cultivates lovingkindness be conditions for lightness, plasticity and wieldiness of body?

3. Can these three qualities also be produced by kamma?

4. What is the function of space?

---

[5]Space in the ear or the nose is space that is not conditioned by one of the four factors of kamma, citta, temperature or nutrition; it is unconditioned rūpa.

Chapter 8

Characteristics of Rūpas

As we have seen, rūpas can be classified as sabhāva rūpas, rūpas with their own distinct nature and asabhāva rūpas, rūpas without their own distinct nature. The four Great Elements are sabhāva rūpas, they each have their own distinct nature and characteristic. Rūpas such as lightness, plasticity and wieldiness are asabhāva rūpas, they are qualities of rūpas. The Dhammasangaṇi (§596) incorporates in the list of the twentyeight kinds of rūpa not only rūpas with their own distinct nature but also qualities of rūpa and characteristics of rūpa.

It mentions four different rūpas which are characteristics of rūpa, lakkhaṇa rūpas (lakkhaṇa means characteristic). These four characteristics common to all sabhāva rūpas are the following:

arising or origination (upacaya)[1]

continuity or development (santati)

decay or ageing (jaratā)

falling away or impermanence (aniccatā)

Rūpas do not arise singly, they arise in different groups (kalāpas). The groups of rūpa arise fall away, but they do not fall away as

---
[1] Literally: initial accumulation.

rapidly as citta. Rūpa lasts as long as the duration of seventeen moments of citta arising and falling away, succeeding one another. After the arising of rūpa there are moments of its presence: its continuity or development. Decay, jaratā rūpa, is the characteristic indicating the moment close to its falling away and impermanence, aniccatā rūpa, is the characteristic indicating the moment of its falling away.

We do not notice that the rūpas of our body fall away and that time and again new rūpas are produced which fall away again. So long as we are alive, kamma, citta, temperature and nutrition produce rūpas and thus our bodily functions can continue. These rūpas arise, develop, decay and fall away within splitseconds.

The "Atthasālinī" (II, Book II, Part I, Ch II, 327) and also the "Visuddhimagga" (Ch XIV, 66, 67) speak in a general, conventional sense about the arising of rūpas at the first moment of life, the initial arising, and they explain that after the initial arising at rebirth there is 'continuity', that is to say, the subsequent arising of the groups of rūpa.

Thus, we have to remember that the characteristics are taught by different methods: according to the very short duration of one rupa that arises and continues before it decays and falls away or in a more general way, in conventional sense.

The characteristics of rūpa are taught in a conventional sense in order to help people to have more understanding of these characteristics of rūpa which denote the arising, the continuity, the decay and the falling away. The teaching was adapted to the capabilities to understand of different people.

The "Atthasālinī" ((II, Book II, Part I, Ch II, 327) explains in a wider sense, by way of conventional terms, the origination of rūpa at the first moment of life and the continuity of rūpa as the subsequent arising of rūpa. Throughout our life there is continuity in the production of rūpa.

We read about continuity:

> "Continuity has the characteristic of continuous
> occurrence, the function of linking or binding without a

break, unbroken series as manifestation, matter bound
up without a break as proximate cause."

This definition of continuity in a more general sense reminds us that the seeming permanence of the body is merely due to the continuous production of new rūpas replacing the ones that have fallen away.

We read in the " Visuddhimagga" (Ch XIV, 68) about decay or ageing:

> " Ageing has the characteristic of maturing (ripening) material instances. Its function is to lead on towards [their termination]. It is manifested as the loss of newness without the loss of individual essence, like oldness in paddy. Its proximate cause is matter that is maturing (ripening). This is said with reference to the kind of ageing that is evident through seeing alteration in teeth, etc., as their brokenness, and so on (cf. Dhs. 644) ... "

The commentary to the Visuddhimagga explains as to the simile of the paddy, that paddy, when it is ageing, becomes harsh, but that it does not lose its nature, that it is still paddy. It states: "The ageing is during the moments of its presence, then that dhamma does not abandon its specific nature."

Thus, here the commentary does not speak in a general, conventional way, but it refers to decay as one of the four characteristics of a single rūpa, to the moment that is close to its falling away. After a rūpa such as visible object has arisen, there are the moments of its presence, it is decaying and then it falls away. It is the same visible object that is present and decaying, it does not lose its specific nature.

The "Atthasālinī" explains terms used by the "Dhammasaṅgaṇi" in reference to decay, such as decrepitude, hoariness, wrinkles, the shrinkage in length of days, the overripeness of the faculties:

> " ... By the word 'decrepitude' is shown the function which is the reason for the broken state of teeth, nails,

etc., in process of time. By hoariness is shown the
function which is the reason for the greyness of hair on
the head and body. By 'wrinkles' is shown the function
which is the reason for the wrinkled state in the skin
making the flesh fade. Hence these three terms show the
function of decay in process of time ... "

As to the terms "shrinkage in life and maturity of faculties", these show the resultant nature of this decay. We read:

" ... Because the life of a being who has reached decay
shortens, therefore decay is said to be the shrinkage in
life by a figure of speech. Moreover, the faculties, such
as sight, etc., capable of easily seizing their own object,
however subtle, and which are clear in youth, are
mature in one who has attained decay; they are
disturbed, not distinct, and not capable of seizing their
own object however gross ... "

When we notice decay of our teeth, wrinkles of the skin and greying of our hairs, decay is obvious. However, we should remember that each rūpa that arises is susceptible to decay, that it will fall away completely.

As to impermanence, aniccatā, the "Visuddhimagga" (Ch XIV, 69) states about it as follows[2] :

"Impermanence of matter has the characteristic of
complete breaking up. Its function is to make material
instances subside. It is manifested as destruction and fall
(cf. Dhs. 645). Its proximate cause is matter that is
completely breaking up."

The commentary to the "Visuddhimagga" speaks about the impermanence as the falling away of each rūpa:

" It is said that its function is to make (material
instances) subside, since this (impermanence) causes the

---

[2] See Dhammasaṅgaṇi §645 and Atthasālinī, II, Book II, Part I, Ch II, 328

materiality that has reached (the moments of) presence as it were to subside. And since this (impermanence), because of the state of dissolution of material phenomena, should be regarded as destruction and fall, it is said that it is manifested as destruction and fall."

As soon as rūpa has arisen, it is led onward to its termination and it breaks up completely, never to come back again. Remembering this is still theoretical knowledge of the truth of impermanence, different from right understanding that realizes the arising and falling away of a nāma or a rūpa. When understanding has not yet reached this stage one cannot imagine what it is like. One may tend to cling to ideas about the arising and falling away of phenomena but that is not the development of understanding. Nāma and rūpa have each different characteristics and so long as one still confuses nāma and rūpa, their arising and falling away cannot be realized. Understanding is developed in different stages and one cannot forego any stage. First there should be a precise understanding of nāma as nāma and of rūpa as rūpa so that the difference between these two kinds of realities can be clearly seen. It is only at a later stage in the development of understanding that the arising and falling away of nāma and rūpa can be directly known.

The "Atthasālinī" (II, Book II, Part I, Ch II, 329) compares birth, decay and death to three enemies, of whom the first leads someone into the forest, the second throws him down and the third cuts off his head. We read:

> " ... For birth is like the enemy who draws him to enter the forest; because he has come to birth in this or that place. Decay is like the enemy who strikes and fells him to earth when he has reached the forest, because the aggregates (khandhas) produced are weak, dependent on others, lying down on a couch. Death is like the enemy who with a sword cuts off the head of him when he is fallen to the ground, because the aggregates having attained decay, have come to destruction of life."

This simile reminds us of the disadvantages of all conditioned realities that do not last and are therefore no refuge. However, so long as understanding (paññā) has not realized the arising and falling away of nāma and rūpa, one does not grasp their danger.

We read in the "Dīghanakhasutta" (Middle Length Sayings II, no. 74) that the Buddha reminded Dīghanakha that the body is susceptible to decay, impermanent and not self:

> "But this body, Aggivessana, which has material shape, is made up of the four great elements, originating from mother and father, nourished on gruel and sour milk, of a nature to be constantly rubbed away, pounded away, broken up and scattered, should be regarded as impermanent, suffering, as a disease, a tumour, a dart, a misfortune, an affliction, as other, as decay, empty, not-self. When he regards this body as impermanent, suffering, as a disease, a tumour, a dart, a misfortune, an affliction, as other, as decay, empty, not-self, whatever in regard to body is desire for body, affection for body, subordination to body, this is got rid of."

Origination, continuity, decay and impermanence are characteristics common to all sabhāva rūpas. They do not have their own distinct nature, thus, they are asabhāva rūpas. These characteristics are not produced by the four factors of kamma, citta, food and temperature. Rūpas have been classified as twentyeight kinds. Summarizing them, they are:

solidity (or extension)

cohesion

temperature

motion

eyesense

earsense

nose (smellingsense)

tongue (tastingsense)

bodysense

visible object

sound

odour

flavour

femininity

masculinity

heart-base

life faculty

nutrition

space

bodily intimation

speech intimation

lightness

plasticity

wieldiness

origination

continuity

decay

impermanence

CHAPTER 8. CHARACTERISTICS OF ALL RŪPAS

Rūpas can be classified as the four Principle Rūpas and the twentyfour derived rūpas. The four Principle rūpas, mahā-bhūta rūpas, are the four Great Elements. The derived rūpas, upādā rūpas, are the other twentyfour rūpas that arise in dependence upon the four Great Elements.

Rūpas can be classified as gross and subtle. As we have seen (in Chapter 4), twelve kinds of rūpa are gross: visible object, sound, odour, flavour and three of the four Great Elements which are tangible object (excluding cohesion), as well as the five sense-organs. They are gross because of impinging: visible object impinges on the eyesense, sound impinges on the earsense, and each of the other sense objects impinges on the appropriate sense-base. The other sixteen kinds of rūpa are subtle. What is subtle is called "far" because it is difficult to penetrate, whereas what is gross is called "near", because it is easy to penetrate (Vis. XIV, 73).

Furthermore, other distinctions can be made. Rūpas can be classified as sabhāva rūpas, rūpas with their own distinct nature, and asabhāva rūpas, rūpas without their own distinct nature. The twelve gross rūpas and six among the subtle rūpas that are: cohesion, nutrition, life faculty, heart-base, femininity and masculinity are rupas each with their own distinct nature and characteristic, they are sabhāva rūpas.

The other ten subtle rūpas do not have their own distinct nature, they are asabhāva rūpas. Among these are the two kinds of intimation, bodily intimation and speech intimation, which are a "certain, unique change" in the eight inseparable rūpas produced by citta. Moreover, the three qualities of lightness, plasticity and weildiness, classified together with the two rūpas of intimation as vikāra rūpas (rūpa as changeability or alteration) are included in the asabhāva rūpas. Furthurmore, the rūpa space (akāsa or pariccheda rūpa) that delimits the groups of rūpa, as well as the four rūpas that are the characteristics of origination, continuity, decay and impermanence, are included.

Rūpas can be classified as produced rūpas, nipphanna rūpas, and unproduced rūpas, anipphanna rūpas. The sabhāva rūpas are also called "produced", whereas the asabhāva rūpas are also called "unproduced"[3]. The two kinds of intimation produced by citta, the three qualities of lightness, plasticity and wieldiness produced by citta, temperature or nutrition and space which delimits the groups of rūpa produced by the four factors and therefore originating from these four factors, are still called "unproduced", anipphanna, because they themselves are not rūpas with their own distinct nature, they are not "concrete matter".

The "produced rūpas" which each have their own characteristic are, as the "Visuddhimagga" (XVIII, 13) explains, "suitable for comprehension", that is, they are objects of which right understanding can be developed. For example, visible object or hardness have characteristics that can be objects of awareness when they appear, and they can be realized by paññā as they are, as non-self. The "unproduced rūpas" are "not suitable for comprehension" since they are qualities of rūpa such as changeability or the rūpa that delimits groups of rūpas. If one does not know this distinction, one may be led to wrong practice.

Questions

1. Can the rūpas of lightness, plasticity and wieldiness be objects of awareness?

---

[3] For details see Visuddhimagga XIV, 73, 77.

Chapter 9

Groups of Rūpas

Rūpas do not arise singly, they always arise collectively, in groups (kalāpas). Where there is solidity, the Element of Earth, there have to be the other three Great Elements, and also colour, flavour, odour and nutrition. These are the eight inseparable rūpas. A group of rūpas consisting of only the eight inseparable rūpas is called a "pure octad". Pure octads of the body are produced by citta, temperature or nutrition, and pure octads outside the body are produced only by temperature.

The groups of rūpas produced by kamma have to consist of at least nine rūpas: the eight inseparable rūpas and life faculty (jīvitindriya), and such a group is called a "nonad". Eyesense, earsense, smelling-sense, tasting-sense, bodysense, heart-base, femininity and masculinity are other kinds of rūpa produced by kamma and each of these rūpas arises together with the eight inseparable rūpas and life faculty, thus, they arise in groups of ten rūpas, decads. All rūpas of such a decad are produced by kamma. Thus, one speaks of eye-decad, ear-decad, nose-decad, tongue-decad, body-decad, heart-base-decad, femininity-decad and masculinity-decad. As to the body-decad, this arises and falls away at any place of the body where there can be sensitivity.

Kamma produces groups of rūpas from the arising moment of the rebirth-consciousness (paṭisandhi-citta). In the case of human beings, kamma produces at that moment the three decads of bodysense, of sex (femininity or masculinity) and of heart-base, and it produces these decads throughout our life. The eye-decad and the decads of ear, nose and tongue are not produced at the first moment of life but later on.

The citta which is rebirth-consciousness does not produce rūpa. The citta which immediately succeeds the rebirth-consciousness, namely the life-continuum (bhavanga-citta)[1] , produces rūpa. One moment of citta can be divided into three extremely short phases: its arising moment, the moment of its presence and the moment of its falling away. Citta produces rūpa at its arising moment, since citta is then strong. At the moment of its presence and the moment of its dissolution it is weak and then it does not produce rūpa (Visuddhimagga XX, 32). When the citta succeeding the rebirth-consciousness, the life-continuum, arises, it produces a pure octad. Later on citta produces, apart from pure octads, also groups with bodily intimation, with speech intimation and with the three rūpas of lightness, plasticity and wieldiness, which always have to arise together. These three kinds of rūpa also arise in a group together with bodily intimation and speech intimation. In the case of speech intimation, also sound arises together with speech intimation in one group.

Throughout life citta produces rūpa, but not all cittas can produce rūpa. As we have seen, the rebirth-consciousness does not produce rūpa. Among the cittas that do not produce rūpa are also the sense-cognitions of seeing, hearing, etc. Seeing only sees, it has no other capacity. Some cittas can produce rūpas but not bodily intimation and speech intimation, and some cittas can produce the two kinds of intimation. Among the cittas that can produce the two kinds of intimation are the kusala cittas of the sense-sphere (thus not those that attain absorption or jhāna and those that realize enlightenment), and the akusala cittas[2].

---
[1]The bhavanga-citta arises in between the processes of cittas; it does not experience objects that impinge on the six doors, but it experiences the same object as the rebirth-consciousness. It maintains the continuity in the life of the individual.

[2]See Visuddhimagga XX, 31, and Atthasālinī II, Book II, Part I, Ch III, 325.

Temperature (heat-element) can produce groups of rūpas of the body as well as groups of rūpas of materiality outside. In the case of materiality outside it produces groups that are "pure octads" and also groups with sound[3]. Rūpas that are not of the body are solely produced by temperature, they are not produced by kamma, citta or nutrition. When we see a rock or plant we may think that they last, but they consist of rūpas originated by temperature, arising and falling away all the time. Rūpas are being replaced time and again, and we do not realize that rūpas which have fallen away never come back.

As regards groups of rūpas of the body, temperature produces pure octads and also groups with lightness, plasticity and wieldiness.

As we have seen, kamma produces rūpa in a living being from the moment the rebirth-consciousness arises. Kamma produces rūpa at each of the three moments of citta: at its arising moment, at the moment of its presence and at the moment of its falling away. In each group of rūpas produced by kamma there is the element of heat (utu), which is one of the four Great Elements, and this begins to produce new rūpas at the moment of presence of rebirth-consciousness, thus, not at the arising moment of rebirth-consciousness. The element of heat produces other rūpas during the moments of its presence, it cannot produce rūpas at its arising moment[4]. It originates a pure octad and from that moment on it produces, throughout life, rūpas during the moments of its presence[5].

---

[3]Sound can be produced by temperature or by citta.

[4]Temperature and nutrition, rūpas which produce other rūpas, do not produce these at the moment of their arising, since they are then weak, but they produce rūpas during the moments of presence, before they fall away. The duration of rūpa, when compared with the duration of citta, is as long as seventeen moments of citta, thus there are fifteen moments of presence of rūpa. Citta, however, produces rūpas at its arising moment since it is then strong.

[5]The heat-element present in a group which is produced by temperature, no matter whether of materiality outside or of the body, can, in its turn, produce a pure octad and in this way several occurrences of octads can be linked up. In the same way, the heat-element present in groups of rūpas of the body, produced by kamma or citta can, in its turn, produce a pure octad, and the heat-element present in that octad can produce another octad, and so on. In this way several occurrences of octads are linked

Nutritive essence present in food that has been swallowed [6], produces rūpas and it supports and sustains the body. Rūpas produced by nutrition arise only in the body of living beings. Nutrition produces pure octads and also groups of rūpa with lightness, plasticity and wieldiness.

Nutritive essense is one of the inseparable rūpas present in each group of rūpas. Nutritive essence in nutriment-originated octads originates a further octad with nutritive essence and thus, it links up the occurrences of several octads. The "Visuddhimagga" (XX, 37) states that nutriment taken on one day can thus sustain the body for as long as seven days[7].

The groups of rūpas produced by kamma, citta, temperature and nutrition are interrelated and support one another. If only kamma would produce rūpas the body could not continue to exist. We read in the "Visuddhimagga" (XVII, 196):

> "... But when they thus give consolidating support to each other, they can stand up without falling, like sheaves of reeds propped up together on all four sides, even though battered by the wind, and like (boats with) broken floats that have found a support, even though battered by waves somewhere in mid-ocean, and they can last one year, two years ... a hundred years, until those beings' life span or their merit is exhausted."

The "Atthasālinī" (I, Book I, Part III, Ch I, 84) [8], in the context of bodily intimation, explains that groups of rūpa produced by citta are interlocked with groups of rūpas produced by kamma, temperature and nutrition. We read:

> When the body set up by mind (citta) moves, does the body set up by the other three causes move or not? The

---

up. Temperature produced by nutrition can also, in its turn, produce another octad.

[6] See Ch 2. The substance of morsel-made food (kabaḷinkāro āhāro) contains nutritive essence, ojā. When food has been swallowed the nutritive essence pervades the body and supports it.

[7] Also nutriment smeared on the body originates materiality, according to the "Visuddhimagga". Some creams, for example, nourish the skin.

[8] See also Visuddhimagga XIV, 61.

latter moves likewise, goes with the former, and invariably follows it. Just as dry sticks, grass, etc., fallen in the flowing water go with the water or stop with it, so should the complete process be understood . . .

The study of the groups of rūpas produced by the four factors of kamma, citta, temperature and nutrition and also their interrelation shows us the complexity of the conditions for the bodily phenomena and functions from birth to death[9]. It reminds us that there is no self who can control the body.

Not all types of rūpa arise in the different planes of existence where living beings are born. Apart from the plane of human beings, there are also other planes of existence. Birth in an unhappy plane or a happy plane is the result of kamma. Birth in the human plane of existence is the result of kusala kamma. During life there are conditions for the occurring of results of kusala kamma and of akusala kamma, namely, the experience of pleasant objects as well as unpleasant objects through the senses. In the human plane the decads of eye, ear, nose, tongue and bodysense that are produced by kamma arise, so that the different sense objects can be experienced. People who see the disadvantages of enslavement to sense impressions and have accumulated the right conditions for the development of a high degree of calm, can attain stages of jhāna. The result of the different stages of jhāna is birth in higher planes of existence where less sense impressions occur or none at all. In some of the higher planes[10] the decads of nose, tongue, bodysense and sex are absent, but the decads of eye and ear, the decad of the heart-base and the nonad of life faculty (life faculty and the eight inseparable rūpas) arise. The rūpas produced by nutrition do not arise. In these planes one does not need food to stay alive.

In one of the higher planes of existence there is no nāma, only

---

[9] For details see: Atthasālinī II, Book II, Part I, Ch III, 342, 343, and Visuddhimagga XX, 32-43.

[10] The rūpa-brahma planes. Birth in these planes is the result of rūpa-jhāna, fine-material jhāna.

rūpa[11]. Here the decads of eye, ear and the other senses, sex and heart-base are absent. Sound does not arise and neither do rūpas produced by citta arise, since nāma does not arise. Kamma produces the nonad of life faculty at the first moment of life and after that also temperature produces rūpas.

In some of the higher planes only nāma ocurs and thus rūpas do not arise in such planes[12].

Questions

1. Can kamma produce groups of eight rūpas, pure octads?

2. Which decads produced by kamma arise at the first moment of life in the case of human beings?

3. Can rebirth-consciousness produce rūpa?

4. Can seeing-consciousness produce rūpa?

5. Can citta rooted in attachment produce rūpa?

---

[11] The "perceptionless beings plane" (asañña-satta plane) which is one of the rūpa-brahma planes. Those who are born here have seen the disadvantages of nāma.

[12] The arūpa-brahma planes. Birth in these planes is the result of arūpa-jhāna, "immaterial jhāna".

Chapter 10

Conclusion

The study of the different kinds of rūpa will help us to understand more clearly the various conditions for the arising of bodily phenomena and mental phenomena. Gradually we shall come to understand that all our experiences in life, all the objects we experience, our bodily movements and our speech are only conditioned nāma and rūpa. In the planes of existence where there are nāma and rūpa, nāma conditions rūpa and rūpa conditions nāma in different ways. The rūpas that are sense objects and the rūpas that can function as sense-doors are conditions for the different cittas arising in processes which experience sense objects.

In order to develop understanding of nāma and rūpa it is necessary to learn to be mindful of the nāma or rūpa appearing at the present moment. Only one object at a time can be object of mindfulness and in the beginning we may find this difficult. The study of rūpas can help us to have more clarity about the fact that only one object at a time can be experienced through one of the six doors. Visible object, for example, can be experienced through the eye-door, it cannot be experienced through the body-door, thus, through touch. Seeing-consciousness experiences what is visible and body-consciousness experiences tangible object, such as hardness or softness. Through each door the appropriate object can be experienced and the different doorways should not be confused with one another.

When we believe that we can see and touch a flower, we think of a concept. We can learn to see the difference between awareness of one reality at a time and thinking of a concept. A concept or conventional truth can be an object of thought, but it is not a paramattha dhamma, an ultimate reality with its own inalterable characteristic.

It may seem difficult to be mindful of one reality at a time, but realities such as visible object, hardness or sound are impinging on the senses time and again. When we have understood that they have different characteristics and that they present themselves one at a time, we can learn to be mindful of them. We should remember that at the moment of mindfulness of a reality understanding of that reality can be developed. Right understanding should be the goal. There is no self who understands. Understanding is a cetasika, a type of nāma; it understands and it can develop.

Right understanding is developed in different stages of insight and it is useful to know more about the first stage. When the first stage of insight has been reached, paññā, understanding, distinguishes the characteristic of nāma from the characteristic of rūpa. In theory we know that nāma experiences something and that rūpa does not experience anything, but when they appear there is, at first, not yet direct understanding of their different characteristics. We may, for example, cling to an idea of "I am feeling hot". What is there in reality? There is nāma that experiences heat and there is rūpa that is heat, but we tend to think of a "whole", a conglomeration of different phenomena: of a person who feels hot. Then nāma cannot be distinguished from rūpa. It is true that when heat is experienced, also the rūpa that is heat is present. However, only one reality at a time can be object of mindfulness. Sometimes nāma is the object of mindfulness and sometimes rūpa, and this depends on conditions. When one reality at a time is object of mindfulness, one does not, at that moment, think of "self" or "my body". Gradually understanding can develop and then clinging to self will decrease. Rūpas impinging on the five senses are experienced through the sense-doors as well as through the mind-door. Nāma cannot be experienced through a sense-door, but only through the mind-door. Each of the sense-objects that is experienced through the appropriate sense-door is also experienced through the mind-door. We may understand that seeing sees visible object, but the experience of visible object through the mind-door is concealed. The processes of cittas pass very rapidly and when understanding has not been developed it is not clearly known what the mind-door process is. At the first stage of insight paññā arising in a mind-door process clearly realizes the difference between the characteristic of nāma and the characteristic of rūpa, and at that stage it is also known what the mind-door is. When understanding develops it will eventually lead to that stage.

The study of nāma and rūpa can clear up misunderstandings about the development of understanding and about the object of understanding. Reading about nāma and rūpa and pondering over them are conditions for the development of right understanding of the realities presenting themselves through the six doors. We read in the "Therīgāthā" (Psalms of the Sisters) about people in the Buddha's time who were disturbed by problems and could not find mental stability. When they were taught Abhidhamma they could develop right understanding and even attain enlightenment. While one studies the elements, the sense-doors, the objects, in short, all ultimate realities (paramattha dhammas), the truth that there is no being or self becomes more evident. We read in Canto 57 about Bhikkhunī[1] Vijayā who could not find peace of mind. After she had been taught Abhidhamma she developed right understanding of realities and attained arahatship [2] We read:

> "Four times, nay five, I sallied from my cell,
>
> And roamed afield to find the peace of mind
>
> I lacked, and governance of thoughts
>
> I could not bring into captivity.
>
> Then to a Bhikkhunī I came and asked
>
> Full many a question of my doubts.
>
> To me she taught Dhamma: the elements,

---
[1] Bhikkhunī means nun or sister.
[2] The fourth and last stage of enlightenment.

Organ and object in the life of sense,
(And then the factors of the Nobler life:)
The Ariyan truths, the Faculties, the Powers,
The Seven Factors of Enlightenment [3],
The Eightfold Path, leading to utmost good.
I heard her words, her bidding I obeyed.
While passed the first watch of the night there rose
Long memories of the bygone line of lives.
While passed the second watch, the Heavenly Eye,
Purview celestial, I clarified [4].
While passed the last watch of the night, I burst
And rent aside the gloom of ignorance.
Then, letting joy and blissful ease of mind
Suffuse my body, seven days I sat,
Ere stretching out cramped limbs I rose again.
Was it not rent indeed, that muffling mist?"

---

[3] The ariyan Truths are the four noble Truths: the Truth of dukkha, that is, the impermanence and unsatisfactoriness of all conditioned realities; the Truth of the origin of dukkha, that is, craving; the Truth of the cessation of dukkha, that is, nibbāna; the Truth of the way leading to the cessation of dukkha, that is, the development of the eightfold Path. The Faculties, Powers, Seven Factors of Enlightenment are wholesome qualities that develop together with satipaṭṭhāna so that enlightenment can be attained. Among them are mindfulness, energy, concentration and understanding.

[4] The Heavenly Eye is the knowledge of the passing away and rebirth of beings.

Glossary

abhidhamma the higher teachings of Buddhism, teachings on ultimate realities.

akāsa space

akusala unwholesome, unskilful.

anāgāmī non returner, person who has reached the third stage of enlightenment, he has no aversion (dosa).

anattā not self.

anicca impermanent

aniccatā falling away or impermanence.

apo-dhātu element of water or cohesion.

arahat noble person who has attained the fourth and last stage of enlightenment.

ārammaṇa object which is known by consciousness.

ariyan noble person who has attained enlightenment.

asabhāva rūpas rūpas without their own distinct nature.

avinibbhoga rūpas the four Great elements and four derived rūpas, which always arise together.

bhikkhu monk.

bhikkhunī nun.

Buddha a fully enlightened person who has discovered the truth all by himself, without the aid of a teacher.

cakkhu-dhātu eye element.

cakkhu-dvāra eyedoor.

cakkhu-viññāṇa seeing-consciousness.

cakkhu eye.

cakkhuppasāda rūpa rūpa which is the organ of eyesense, capable of receiving visible object.

cetanā volition or intention.

cetasika mental factor arising with consciousness.

citta consciousness, the reality which knows or cognizes an object.

dassana-kicca function of seeing.

dhamma-dhātu element of dhammas, realities, comprising cetasikas, subtle rūpas, nibbāna.

dhamma reality, truth, the teachings.

dhammārammaṇa all objects other than the sense objects which can be experienced through the five sense-doors, thus, objects which can be experienced only through the mind-door.

Dhātukathā Discourse on the Elements, the third book of the Abhidhamma.

diṭṭhi wrong view, distorted view of realities.

dukkha suffering, unsatisfactoriness of conditioned realities.

dvāra doorway through which an object is experienced, the five sense-doors or the mind door.

dvi-pañca-viññāṇa the five pairs of sense-cognitions, which are seeing, hearing, smelling, tasting and body-consciousness. Of each pair one is kusala vipāka and one akusala vipāka.

ghāna-dhātu nose element.

ghāna-viññāṇa smelling-consciousness.

ghānappasāda rūpa rūpa which is the organ of smelling sense, capable of receiving odour.

ghāyana-kicca function of smelling.

hadayavatthu heart-base.

itthindriyaṃ femininity-faculty.

jaratā decay or ageing.

jivhā-dhātu tongue element.

jivhāppasāda rūpa rūpa which is the organ of tasting sense, capable of receiving flavour.

jivhā-viññāṇa tasting-consciousness.

jīvitindriya life faculty.

kāma sensual enjoyment or the five sense objects.

kamma patha course of action performed through body, speech or mind which can be wholesome or unwholesome.

kamma intention or volition; deed motivated by volition.

kammaññatā wieldiness.

kāya-dhātu the element of bodysense.

kāya-viññatti bodily intimation, such as gestures, facial expression, etc.

kāya-viññāṇa body-consciousness.

kāya body. It can also stand for the mental body, the cetasikas.

kāyappasāda rūpa bodysense, the rūpa which is capable of receiving tangible object. It is all over the body, inside or outside.

khandhas conditioned realities classified as five groups: physical phenomena, feelings, perception or remembrance, activities or formations (cetasikas other than feeling or perception), consciousness.

kicca function.

kusala citta wholesome consciousness.

kusala kamma a good deed.

kusala wholesome, skilful

lahutā buoyancy or lightness.

Mahā-bhūta rūpas the four Great Elements

moha ignorance.

mudutā plasticity.

nāma mental phenomena.

nibbāna unconditioned reality, the reality which does not arise and fall away. The destruction of lust, hatred and delusion. The deathless. The end of suffering.

oḷārika rūpas gross rūpas (sense objects and sense organs).

ojā the rūpa which is nutrition.

paṭhavī-dhātu The element of earth.

paṭisandhi-citta the first moment of life the rebirth-consciousness.

Pāli the language of the Buddhist teachings.

paññā wisdom or understanding.

paññatti concepts, conventional terms.

paramattha dhamma truth in the absolute sense: including citta, cetasika, rūpa and nibbāna.

pariccheda rūpa the rūpa that is space, delimiting the groups of rūpa (pariccheda meaning limit or boundary).

pasāda-rūpas rūpas which are capable of receiving sense-objects such as visible object, sound, taste, etc.

Purisindriyaṃ masculinity-faculty.

rūpa physical phenomena, realities which do not experience anything.

sabhāva rūpas rūpas with their own distinct nature.

saddārammaṇa sound.

saṅkhata or saṅkhāra dhamma conditioned dhamma.

saññā-kkhandha remembrance classified as one of the five khandhas.

saññā memory, remembrance or perception.

santati continuity or development.

saṅkhāra dhamma conditioned dhamma.

sati mindfulness or awareness: non-forgetfulness of what is wholesome, or non-forgetfulness of realities which appear.

satipaṭṭhāna applications of mindfulness. It can mean the cetasika sati which is aware of realities or the objects of mindfulness which are classified as four applications of mindfulness: Body, Feeling, Citta, Dhamma. Or it can mean the Path the Buddha and the aryan disciples have developed.

savana-kicca function of hearing.

sāyana-kicca function of tasting.

sīla morality in action or speech, virtue.

sota-dhātu element of earsense.

sota-dvāra-vīthi-cittas ear-door process cittas.

sota-dvārāvajjana-citta ear-door-adverting-consciousness.

sotāpanna person who has attained the first stage of enlightenment, and who has eradicated wrong view of realities.

sota-viññāṇa hearing-consciousness.

sukhuma rūpas subtle rūpas

sutta part of the scriptures containing dialogues at different places on different occasions.

suttanta a sutta text.

tejo-dhātu element of fire or heat.

Theravāda Buddhism Doctrine of the Elders, the oldest tradition of Buddhism.

Tipiṭaka the teachings of the Buddha.

upacaya arising or origination.

upādā-rūpa derived rūpas, the rūpas other than the four Great Elements.

vacī viññatti speech intimation.

vatthu base, physical base of citta.

vāyo-dhātu element of wind or motion.

viññāṇa consciousness, citta.

vipākacitta citta which is the result of a wholesome deed (kusala kamma) or an unwholesome deed (akusala kamma). It can arise as rebirth-consciousness, or during life as the experience of pleasant or unpleasant objects through the senses, such as seeing, hearing, etc.

vipassanā wisdom which sees realities as they are.

Other books written by Nina van Gorkom

The Buddha's Path An Introduction to the doctrine of Theravada Buddhism.

Buddhism in Daily Life A general introduction to the main ideas of Theravada Buddhism.

Abhidhamma in Daily Life is an exposition of absolute realities in detail. Abhidhamma means higher doctrine and the book's purpose is to encourage the right application of Buddhism in order to eradicate wrong view and eventually all defilements.

The World in the Buddhist Sense The purpose of this book is to show that the Buddhas Path to true understanding has to be developed in daily life.

The Perfections Leading to Enlightenment The Perfections is a study of the ten good qualities: generosity, morality, renunciation, wisdom, energy, patience, truthfulness, determination, loving-kindness, and equanimity.

Cetasikas Cetasika means 'belonging to the mind'. It is a mental factor which accompanies consciousness (citta) and experiences an object. There are 52 cetasikas. This book gives an outline of each of these 52 cetasikas and shows the relationship they have with each other.

The Buddhist Teaching on Physical Phenomena A general introduction to physical phenomena and the way they are related to each other and to mental phenomena.

Books translated by Nina van Gorkom

Metta: Loving kindness in Buddhism An introduction to the basic Buddhist teachings of metta, loving kindness, and its practical application in todays world.

Taking Refuge in Buddhism Taking Refuge in Buddhism is an introduction to the development of insight meditation.

A Survey of Paramattha Dhammas A Survey of Paramattha Dhammas is a guide to the development of the Buddha's path of wisdom, covering all aspects of human life and human behaviour, good and bad.

These and other articles can be seen at:
www.zolag.co.uk or www.scribd.com (search for zolag).

www.ingramcontent.com/pod-product-compliance
Lightning Source LLC
Chambersburg PA
CBHW031159160426
43193CB00008B/435